Through My Eyes

Vendon Wright

authorHOUSE®

AuthorHouse™ UK Ltd.
1663 Liberty Drive
Bloomington, IN 47403 USA
www.authorhouse.co.uk
Phone: 0800.197.4150

© 2014 Vendon Wright. All rights reserved.

No part of this book may be reproduced, stored in a retrieval system, or transmitted by any means without the written permission of the author.

Published by AuthorHouse 07/24/2014

ISBN: 978-1-4969-8635-1 (sc)
ISBN: 978-1-4969-8636-8 (e)

Any people depicted in stock imagery provided by Thinkstock are models, and such images are being used for illustrative purposes only.
Certain stock imagery © Thinkstock.

Because of the dynamic nature of the Internet, any web addresses or links contained in this book may have changed since publication and may no longer be valid. The views expressed in this work are solely those of the author and do not necessarily reflect the views of the publisher, and the publisher hereby disclaims any responsibility for them.

CONTENTS

About the book vii
A Guide to Retinitis Pigmentosa xi

1 The disappearing world 1
2 I can see ghosts 10
3 The Art of guessing 19
4 Open your eyes 25
5 Let the fight begin 30
6 Suffering in silence 35
7 Living with my disability 39
8 Through my eyes 49
9 You are blessed 54
10 I'm not a robot 64
11 Down but not out 71
12 I'm blessed too 77
13 Now I can see 82

About The Author 91

ABOUT THE BOOK

When I was six years old I started wearing glasses to correct my short sight. My view of my low vision quickly changed when I was twenty years old and found out that my brother had suddenly gone blind. He was told that he was suffering from Retinitis Pigmentosa - RP, a disorder that slowly destroys the pigment cells in the eyes. There are three different strains of RP and the one my brother has runs in the male line of a family. So far, there are no known cures. My brother's eyes deteriorated quickly which confused us all. I soon became curious and convinced myself to attend an eye appointment to determine whether there was more wrong with my eyes than just being short sighted. At the tender age of twenty-one I was also diagnosed with RP. Since then I have been slowly going blind, not knowing when my world would finally fade away forever. Finally at the age of twenty-eight I was also registered blind. Battling against such a crippling disease led me through a labyrinth of challenges. Having to constantly adapt my lifestyle to fit the changes to my vision became almost unbearable. My fight to remain positive was put under yet more pressure when I found out that I was also suffering from Ushers syndrome, a disorder that results in both loss of hearing and of sight.

During my journey I experienced a wide range of emotions as I fought to find a way to deal with my disability. After a long hard battle, overcoming huge obstacles, I finally learnt to embrace my medical condition.

Despite the problems it has caused me, I have managed to keep a positive attitude towards life. I hold a 4th degree Black belt in Taekwondo and I was the first registered blind person in England to achieve this level of excellence. After studying Taekwondo for over twenty years, I now teach many classes of my own. At present I have taught forty of my students to become Black Belts.

The inspiration to write a book came from consistently and persistently helping my friends to overcome their problems. Now I would like to help other people by passing on my strengths. My book is aimed at both the sighted and visually impaired as it gives positive inspirations on handling a variety of problems. It also gives an excellent medical history of RP and how to handle going blind.

Email info@thewrightchoice.co.uk

INTRODUCTION

My name is Vendon Aston Wright. I was born on the sixth of August 1966 in a small town called Rugby in England. Generally, people think that the most interesting aspect of the town is that it is the home of the game Rugby Football.

I have two children named Michaela and Jasmine. I'm registered blind and so is one of my brothers. We have a rare genetically developed eye disorder called Retinitis Pigmentosa (RP) and at present there are no known cures. So far one in three thousand people suffer from RP. I teach a Martial Art called Taekwondo, which is a sport that is featured in the Olympics.

I attained a 4th Degree Black Belt Master of Taekwondo and I was the first registered blind person in England to achieve this level of excellence. This book shows some of the challenges that visually impaired people have to deal with on a daily basis. I explain what it feels like to see the world through a blind person's eyes. Hopefully it will motivate people to see a positive side to their problems and it may also encourage people to appreciate what they can see.

Several character names have been changed to protect the privacy of the people involved.

This book is a tribute to the loving memory of Carline Wright, who passed away on Friday 6 June 2003, aged 46.

A GUIDE TO RETINITIS PIGMENTOSA

You may have been told recently or you have known for some years that you have Retinitis Pigmentosa (RP). This diagnosis could well help to explain the months or years of not being able to see properly in the dark – called night blindness, and of falling over objects which you did not see. You will possibly have been told that, at present, there is no cure for RP and that you have to face the prospect of slowly deteriorating sight. Slow loss of sight is a difficult disability to live with, especially as you may not receive the immediate sympathy and understanding usually shown to the totally blind. Indeed many people will not believe that you have a loss of sight because you have no obvious sign of visual impairment. The first and hardest step towards living positively with a disability is accepting it. If you have RP this means knowing the limitation of your vision and learning to use intelligently the visual clues you still receive. Accepting that you have RP will not be easy. You may go through periods of despair and of feeling resentful, bewildered or even angry. All these reactions are understandable, especially as the very nature of this disorder makes adjustment difficult but the way in which you deal with it determines the type of life you and your family will share from day to day. RP can manifest itself in many ways since it is not one disorder but many with similar symptoms. For some, the loss of sight is slow and there may be only a small loss over perhaps ten years or more. Others have periods of rapid loss, often with years in between with no apparent decline. A person experiencing the early stages of RP may have almost perfect day vision but at night, in brilliant sunshine or in rapidly changing light conditions, the same person may react as if they are almost totally blind. Retinitis Pigmentosa is a group of hereditary disorders whose common feature is a gradual deterioration of the light sensitive cells of the Retina. The symptoms of this group of disorders usually become apparent between the ages of 10 and 30, although some changes may become apparent in childhood. There are many syndromes associated with RP, which result in multiple loss, such as Usher syndrome, in which sight and hearing are both affected.

For more information on RP
www.brps.org.uk

CHAPTER 1

The disappearing world

At the age of twenty years old I found out that my brother had suddenly gone blind. We were told that he was suffering from Retinitis Pigmentosa (RP), which is an eye disorder that slowly destroys the pigment cells in the eyes. There are three different strains of RP and the one my brother has runs in the male line of a family. So far, there are no cures. My brother's eyes deteriorated quickly which confused us all. I soon became curious – scared, and persuaded myself to arrange an eye examination.

I really thought that I was just badly short-sighted and extremely clumsy. My clumsiness increased at night time but being young and naive I ignored all the early signs.

My appointment at the Birmingham Eye Hospital finally came through when I was twenty-one years old. (What a great 21st birthday present I was about to receive!) My appointment was at the same Eye Hospital as my brother Brian. None of my other brothers and sisters were interested in finding out whether they had any serious eye problems so I travelled alone. Birmingham was just half an hour from Rugby by train. Before I got to Birmingham I began to get quite emotional. Tears trickled out of my eyes in sadness for my brother who I was so close to. I remember saying that I wished that I had the eye disorder instead of him because he was in the middle of studying at college. There is an old saying, 'Be careful what you wish for'; I was about to find out that it is good advice.

When I got to Birmingham I looked at my ticket to see which one to give to the ticket collector. Although it was a little difficult, I managed to see which one said 'Out' and which one said 'Return'. In a short while I would find out how important little bits of information are. I then set out to find my destination.

The Eye Hospital wasn't far from the train station, so was not too hard to find. I loved shopping in Birmingham so I decided I'd have a look around the shops on my way back. Dodging around a few boulders and crossing two roads, I finally found the hospital.

After finding the reception and registering myself in, I sat down to await my fate. It seemed ages before I heard my name so I had time to look around. Was I in the right place? Most of the people waiting were old.

"Imagine if I end up like them needing assistance to get around," I thought to myself.

Finally my name was called and I entered the room.

I was asked to read from the chart and I got down to the third line but I struggled more with my left eye. I remember thinking to myself that I would have to be blind if I was unable to see the big huge letter at the top.

"Thank you Mr Wright, you may return to your seat to await the next test."

I thought for a moment; "Maybe it's time you asked some questions about the tests you're going through."

So I prepared myself.

"Was that good?" I asked.

"That's fine," he said.

"Where should I be able to read to?"

I was a little shocked by the answer.

"All the way to the bottom of the chart."

At this point I was on my feet.

"All the way to the bottom!" I thought, walking towards the chart on the wall.

Through My Eyes

The writing was ridiculously too small for me to read even when I was standing directly in front of the chart.

"I thought that the last few lines were for people who are long-sighted," I said.

I stood right next to the chart, looking at the last line in amazement.

"How are people supposed to read that?"

I took a long look at it and then left with more questions starting to rush around my head.

"Why don't my glasses correct my sight enough to see everything?"

More and more questions filled my mind and before long I was called for my next test.

I was put in a dark room with what looked like a satellite dish in the middle.

"Cool, I'm going to watch TV!" I thought.

I was asked to take my glasses off and a sticky patch was put on my left eye. I sat with my chin on a chin rest looking into the centre of the dish. It was about the same size as a satellite dish and was white with a black dot in the middle. I later found out that it was not a black dot; it was a small lens so they could see my eye movements in the test that the doctor was about to start. He then explained what he was going to do. He said that he was going to shine a small light onto the dish, and I had to keep looking at the centre while clicking a little beeper whenever I could see the light.

"This sounds like fun," I thought to myself.

For the next ten minutes I played the game, pressing the beeper every time I saw the light. I noticed though that on several occasions the doctor stopped and asked me to make sure that I was pressing it every time I saw the light. He also swapped the little light for a bigger one so that I could see it a little more clearly.

We went on to test my left eye. When we had finished he asked me if I was okay. I replied that I was, but that I needed him to explain why the light kept disappearing on certain parts of the dish. Maybe I would have been better off not asking questions.

"The light was disappearing where your eye has blind spots," he said and continued to explain that the light was always there.

"Blind spots?" I asked.

"Yes Mr Wright, there are parts of your eyes that cannot see anything."

"Blind... spots?" I repeated.

"That dish is like your field of vision. If you were outside, it means that if there was something in the field of your blind spots you physically would not see it."

He then put some eye drops in my eyes to dilate the pupils.

"The drops will open up your eyes so that we can take a good look into them," the doctor explained.

Then he asked me to wait in the waiting room for the eye drops to take effect.

More questions, more thoughts raced around my mind while I was in the waiting room, waiting for my eyes to fully dilate.

"I wonder, is this why the football and cricket ball kept disappearing like magic when I was at school? Is this why the tennis ball seemed to travel at different speeds almost like it had a mind of its own? Could this be why things on the TV screen seem to appear from nowhere? What's happening to me?"

My thoughts escalated.

"Could this be why words in books seem to become invisible just after I've read them?"

Question after question went around my head. It seemed to take forever to be called in for the next test. I noticed that everything around me slowly became more and more blurred. The room also seemed to be getting brighter as if I could see more in places where I thought there were shadows.

The next test was upon me. The doctor looked into my eyes with a bright light called an ophthalmoscope, asking me to look left, look right, up and down. He even held my eyelids open with his fingers because at this stage the light was really hurting me and I was struggling to keep my eyes open. Tears were also now streaming down my face. I was given a tissue to wipe them and then he continued with his tests. Did I dare to ask any more questions at this stage? I mean, how much worse could this get? It struggled to come out but I finally asked.

"Can you see anything?"

Maybe I shouldn't have asked, but I was here and I wanted to know what was going on in my eyes.

"Yes, I can see," he replied. "The backs of your eyes seem to be scarred – dark spots where pigments of your eyes have died."

"Died? Dark spots? Blind spots?" I asked.

"Maybe I've died, or maybe I wish I was dead," I thought to myself.

He then put my chin on another chin rest without my glasses on and a machine put a small lens really close to my eyes. It was fluorescent blue and looked just like a colourful contact lens.

"Was that just touching my eyes?" I asked.

"Yes," he replied. "I held your eyes open so that you couldn't blink while this was testing the pressure of your eyes."

"I take it that everything is fine in there?" I asked sarcastically.

"No," he replied.

"Well there's a surprise," I answered.

He said that there was a bit of pressure on my eyes and that I would have to use special eye drops to control it. He went on to ask me if I did anything that involved straining myself.

"Yes," I replied.

"What do you do?"

"I do weight training quite seriously. I lift up very heavy weights two or three times a week."

"I strongly recommend against doing that," he stated.

"Why?"

"It puts too much pressure on your fragile eyes. It will damage your eyes faster."

"What are you saying?" I asked. "I love doing weight training, love it to bits," I said, the disappointment clear in my voice.

"You'll have to do light training only, cardiovascular; that is if you want to extend the life span of your eyes," he replied.

I went out of the room to wait for the final test.

"One more to go," I thought. "If this gets any worse I think I'm going to have a heart attack," I moaned.

A vivid thought came to me.

"Something is wrong, I can feel it, I can sense it."

I sat and waited.

"Something's not right. How can someone who is just short-sighted have so many problems? How could I have so many problems without..."

And then it came to me.

"Unless I have RP."

I sat bolt upright in my seat. "Does that mean I'm going to go... blind?" I cried.

The thought overpowered me.

"My God, what have I done to deserve this punishment?" I asked but no answer came from above.

"Am I cursed... is our family cursed?" I moaned.

"Did I do wrong to someone? What am I going to do if I have got RP and... wait a minute... didn't I say that I wished that I had it instead of Brian?"

A single thought came out of my clouded mind.

"So does that mean that he can see again?"

"If not then life sucks!" I bellowed inside.

At long last I was called into the room for my last test. At this stage I was bumping into everything. The eye drops had fully dilated my pupils and everywhere looked ridiculously distorted. I became dizzy and disorientated. One of the doctors had to lead me into the room like I was an invalid.

"I'm a young, fit man," I thought to myself.

"How could a young, fit, good-looking, tough man need help and assistance like a seventy year old?"

The final test was the worst test of them all. Well, they had to save the best till last! They put a big contact lens in both of my eyes. They were so big that they prevented me from closing my eyelids. Also, to prevent me from blinking, they administered some different eye drops to slow down my automatic reaction of blinking. I felt like my eyes were permanently prized open and were going to explode. I kept feeling as though I should be blinking, but nothing happened; my eyes just stayed open. Then I had to sit there for ten minutes or so while they flashed all sorts of lights and colours into my eyes. I wanted to blink so badly, but obviously it was just not happening.

"Lucky I don't suffer from epilepsy!" I thought as I continued to observe the bright and colourful lights.

My eyes were now hurting really badly as if someone had punched them, or like I hadn't slept for days or I had been crying for a very long time, but being punched would have been easy compared to this. The pain in my eyes was getting too much and the tears were now streaming. I wanted to blink so badly. It was like having cramp but not being able to straighten your joints to relax your muscles.

"I can't bear this any more," I thought to myself.

I could feel my eyes reacting to some of the different contrasts of light, but was still unable to blink. The test seemed to go on forever, but finally it was over and the room lights came back on. I could still see the colours like a rainbow before my eyes. For a while afterwards I still couldn't blink properly. My eyelids still felt too heavy and when I did manage to blink it was slow and sluggish.

"I bet I look like a big baby, sitting here crying," I thought as I wiped my eyes with a tissue.

I returned to my seat to await the results.

The doctor called me into his room. I sat there for a few minutes while he observed the results on the sheets of paper laid out before him. He got up and asked if he could look into my eyes with yet another light.

"Yeah, why not? Everyone else has," I replied as he turned off the overhead light.

After a few more minutes he switched the lights back on and returned to his seat.

"Give me the good news then," I pleaded.

"Well, I'm afraid it's not good news Mr Wright."

"Really," I replied patronisingly.

"I'm afraid that you too have RP."

"Surprise, surprise," I replied with a little humour that I squeezed out of a crying body.

He went back through all the tests and explained how they came to their conclusion. He explained that the last test with all the different flashing lights was to determine which colours I could see in different shades of light.

"Your eyes are struggling with some colours," he said. "They're not responding to many colours in the dark; this means that you suffer from night blindness."

This was all too much for me now. I was overwhelmed with information so I just sat there in silence as he read out my death sentence.

"You and your brother have a rare eye disorder called Retinitis Pigmentosa – RP," he continued. "You inherited it from your father or mother and unfortunately there are no known cures. It will get worse as you get older and you will probably go blind."

"What a great future I have to look forward to," I thought to myself.

"We will have to monitor you on a regular basis. This will also help us to understand your condition more and maybe in the future we will develop a cure."

He then asked me a few questions about my job. I told him that I was a computer technician working in front of a computer screen all day.

"That's great," he said. "It's the perfect job to be in."

"Why?" I asked waiting for some good news.

"Because you'll be able to see your eyes getting worse so you can monitor them yourself."

"Great," I responded with whatever sarcastic strength I had left.

I sat in anticipation of any more news.

"I have a little good news," he muttered as he reached into his desk. "I'm going to register you as partially sighted so that you can start getting the help that you will need."

He reached over and showed me where to sign.

"Are there any more questions?" he added.

"No," I replied.

I had an information overload. I just wanted to get out of there as quickly as possible. I wanted to crawl under a stone and stay there… forever.

CHAPTER 2

I can see ghosts

The stairs had gone. On the way to my appointment things came naturally so there wasn't much thought to steps and signs. Suddenly I wished that I had memorised my surroundings because with the drops in my eyes that dilated them, I was getting a sneak preview of what it's like to be blind.

Everywhere was blurred, or should I say, more blurred than before.

"Let me think," I thought to myself. "The bright parts are probably the walls so that dark spot must be the stairs."

Luckily I was right, but that was just the beginning of my tortuous journey home. I got to the stairs and looked, and then looked again.

"Who's taken away the steps? How am I supposed to get back down?"

I slowly moved my foot to where I thought the stairs started until I felt the floor disappear. Then I carefully made my way down the stairs. My next task was to try and find the right way out. From where I was standing everywhere looked the same – blurred. So I used my hands to feel around until I found my way out. As I got to the entrance I remembered that there were some more little steps. They were gone too and only a smooth block was left. Using my hands to hold on to the sides of the doorway,

Through My Eyes

I slowly walked to the edge. One of my feet felt the edge of the first step so all I had to do now was walk down them until I ran out of steps. I eventually found my way outside to the street only to find my next challenge.

As I stepped outside I was met by the blinding bright light of the sun. It was incredible, so bright, and it was hurting my eyes so much that I could hardly keep them open.

"What have they done to my eyes?" was my first thought.

I stood there for a short while contemplating what to do. I first took off my glasses to see if the view was any better, but was shocked to discover that everything looked the same with or without my glasses on. I checked once more, first putting them on and then taking them off again, but the images I saw were the same. I decided to leave my glasses on and think of another solution. I looked down at the ground that now looked smooth without any cracks or potholes, and realised that I could withstand the light that was beaming down from the sun. I took a moment to look around and see what the world looked like through my temporary eyes. People looked like ghosts with the sharpness of their images distorted. It was as though they were walking around with masks on their faces. Their faces had no eyes. There was no sign of eyelids, eyelashes or glasses. I couldn't tell if someone had a big nose or a small one and their lips were an occasionally distorted line of red without a distinct difference in shape. If anyone had spots or blackheads then they were invisible to me. Their bodies were a long line of untouched colour but of slightly different thickness. The shoes on their feet blended in with the bottoms of their trousers. I could just make out their hair so I could sometimes guess whether they were male or female, but at this stage I didn't really care. I just wanted to go home and cry. I did think about going back into the Eye Hospital, but this was new to me. I was used to being independent. Imagine having to rely on others to get around, having to ask them to do everything for you and putting your trust in them. I was not ready to accept that I was disabled.

"How do other blind people get around? They must be amazing, or mad."

I started on my way on this narrow pavement that appeared to be very uneven walking in the direction that I thought was the right way to the train station. I bumped into a signpost that seemed to jump into my way. "Who put that there?" I asked myself.

I slowly walked on, being even more cautious. Nothing was clear, not people, buildings, roads or cars.

"Have they moved the pavement?" I wondered. I stopped to observe the entire mass of blob-like shapes that had taken over my horizon. I kept trying to make some sense of what I was seeing.

"I guess those big moving blobs that look like huge stones are cars and buses," I imagined.

The sound of the rushing traffic got louder and louder so I knew I was coming to the point where I would have to cross the road. There was no crossing here so I waited very patiently. I stood for a while studying the movement of the traffic in my new world. I knew this was going to be a test of life or death. I began to rely more and more on my hearing, or what hearing I had left anyway. I'm totally deaf in my right ear so it was incredibly difficult to concentrate on hearing traffic from my right side. It felt easier to judge the traffic when I turned my head to the right so my left ear was to the road. My timing of the cars was also getting better, but I struggled with the silent ghosts. These were people on bicycles. They almost seemed to be coming out of nowhere.

"Do I take the risk and cross?" I thought as I watched the movement of the traffic once more.

I saw a ghost crossing, but by the time I had plucked up the courage to ask for help, they were gone. Most people looked like they were in too much of a hurry so I decided that I was going to have to do it by myself. I waited for a big enough gap between the blobs. At one point it almost went silent and nothing was moving apart from a small blob in the distance. I timed it and it was silent for about eight seconds before the rush of cars and buses came past me. I decided that I was going to go on the next silent gap. The time came and I held my breath as I crossed hesitantly. The blobs became bigger quite fast so I quickened my pace across the road. When I got to the other side I quickly took a guess where the pavement started and almost leapt onto it.

"I made it!" I cried out with astonishment. "I must have been mad to take that risk. I could have been knocked over and killed."

I then got ready for my next challenge.

Once again I stopped and looked around and tried to make some sense of what I was seeing. I saw some green, a white patch then another green patch. I worked out that the green was the grass and the white patch was a path so I walked onto the pure white patch, but then I felt a bump.

"What was that?" I wondered while rubbing my right knee.

"It's a post just stuck in the middle of the path! Someone obviously likes to place posts in the middle of paths without considering people with poor vision," I muttered.

I then slapped it with one of my hands like it was a naughty post and walked on cautiously following the path to the end. As I got to the other end, I suddenly stopped as my mind went back to the post I had just bumped into.

"Maybe there's a post on this side waiting to hit me in my groin," I thought as I moved to the side to avoid a confrontation.

I looked carefully and yes, there it was, just waiting to assault me.

Then I walked along the level path until I met the main road in the City Centre.

"I guess I won't be having a look around town after all," I thought, as I looked left and right to try to work out where I was.

There were so many ghosts around to observe. It was like everyone was wearing almost the same outfits – there were no details to pick out. I took a good look around at my surroundings.

"Everywhere and everything is so blurred that I would be mad to try and walk around town looking in shops."

Then I slowly walked on my way towards the train station, trying to avoid bumping into the mass of ghosts that were obviously in a hurry.

The dazzling light from the sun was still irritating my eyes to such a degree that they were almost closed and streaming with tears of pain. The thoughts of me going blind were beginning to grow once more in my mind.

"What has happened to me?" I cried to myself. "All the beauty of the world has gone and left a view of detail-less images that are so badly distorted that I can't see anything."

Shortly I came to a set of traffic lights that appeared to have no lights so I waited with the ghosts. While waiting to cross the road I contemplated on how I would get across.

"I think my best option would be to just trust everyone else and cross when they cross. Surely we won't all get knocked over," I thought as I prepared to hold my breath again.

It worked and I got across safely. The pavement dipped slightly so I didn't trip but I stumbled a bit as I lifted my leg high to get onto a pavement that wasn't there.

"I bet I looked ridiculous lifting my foot high like a horse," I thought as I walked on as if I hadn't done anything unusual.

"I know where to go but I can't see my way."

I stopped and tried to work out what to do.

"I'll follow people who are going in my direction. If I follow in their footsteps then I shouldn't get assaulted by any more posts."

I began to follow a ghost as if I was a stalker, thinking that they would avoid posts so I should be safe walking behind them. I continued in the direction that I needed to go in and when they walked too fast, I just found someone else slower to follow.

When I got into the bullring where the train station is I hesitated and eventually stopped following people for a while. I became disorientated. The ground looked like it was moving and with the different patterns on the floor it looked like there were small steps everywhere. I stopped to think, but could not remember if there were any little steps. After a while I continued, but kept picking my feet up high as if to go up a step.

I walked even slower now, observing the large blobs which were shops, until I saw a large space where the blob looked completely different, which I assumed was the escalator that would lead down to the train station. I observed my surroundings for a few seconds while I looked to see where all the ghostly figures were going. Over to my right I saw them disappearing downwards so I guessed that must be the escalator I was looking for. I walked even slower towards it knowing that at any second I too could be on it, but if I wasn't prepared for it I would surely trip and have a nasty fall.

"How am I going to step onto an escalator that I can't see and has no separations between the steps?"

They were all the same colour so looked like one continuous blur. Once again I thought that I must be mad to attempt this, as I edged forward even more. I know that I was wrong to feel this way, but I felt too embarrassed to ask for assistance because this was all too new to me and I was used to doing things for myself, so I got ready to take the risk.

"I'm going to take a big step like when I was going onto the pavement and also hold on for good luck!" I thought (well actually it was just in case I fell flat on my face). I picked up my foot to get ready then hopped slightly forward to ensure that I got on. It worked and I was on, but now the steps began to separate quite fast and I think my feet were on two steps so I had to choose really quickly before I slipped down a step or two. It was a little shaky, but I was safe for a moment as the long escalator continued its journey downwards.

"I lost my balance for a second or two, but I did it. Now when do I get off?" was the next thought that came to me.

My heart began to beat faster as I became more nervous.

"I'll take a big step and almost jump as the escalator begins to straighten again."

After a moment I felt the steps beginning to straighten so I got ready and…

"I made it again!" I thought with happiness.

I followed some ghosts that were going in the right direction and observed what they were doing. I saw them stop at a post and move their arm towards it. However, as I got closer I realised that it wasn't a post, it was a ticket collector, but when I reached into my pocket I pulled out several different cards that now all looked the same. "Why didn't I keep it in a separate pocket? I must remember to do that in future," I thought as I looked long and hard for the ticket. I handed him the wrong card a few times before finding the correct one.

After receiving the correct information about my train without asking for more assistance in finding the train, I made my own way over to the platform. I walked up close to where the number of the platform was displayed and was happy to be able to read it. The numbers were about a foot in height.

When I got to the steps I was happy to see that they were bright with dark strips on the edges of each step, so even though I was feeling dizzy from the unexplainable blurred vision, I was able to hold onto the side and walk carefully down to the train platform. I then stood around waiting for my train to arrive.

A train was coming towards me. I wondered if this could be my train. It stopped with a loud screech and I approached the door with caution. I had vivid flashes of a large gap between the train and the platform and the last thing I wanted to do was fall at this stage when I was nearly home. I looked at the edge of the platform and a blob that I hoped was the floor of the train and once again took a big step up. Success! I was now on the train and attempted to look for a seat. Many of the other ghosts had already boarded the train with no mercy for others like me or for people with pushchairs. I began to walk to the left passing what looked like empty seats. I will never be sure whether they really were empty, but that is what I thought at the time. The seats were light blue with a dark blue background and made up of tiny squares – that's not what I saw though. I walked and I stopped, then I walked again until I felt confident enough to sit down. I wouldn't have minded sitting on a young lady's lap, but luckily for her I sat in an empty seat! I stared out of the window as the train started on its journey.

As the train approached Rugby I stayed in my seat until the train came completely to a stop.

"How am I going to open a door when I can't see any handle?"

My next worry was how to get to the door. I decided to look out for someone else getting off at my stop first then follow them. They could then open the door that appeared to have no handle. I was lucky, someone opened the door so I followed them, slightly bumping into seats on the way out. At the entrance to the door I noticed that it seemed much higher than the platform outside.

"Not steps again. I hope that I don't fall between the gap," I thought as I prepared myself to jump once more.

I leapt off the train and landed on the platform.

"I can't believe it! I made it back to Rugby!" I thought with relief.

Some people rushed this way, and some rushed that way.

"Where am I on this platform though?" I asked myself.

Nothing was clear so I guessed left and started walking. Then I stopped and decided to go to the right for a while. I followed someone and soon found that I was on my way out of the station.

When I got to the exit I waited for a while before, yes, following someone else in the new direction that I needed. I didn't live more than five minutes from the station so I thought that I would be fine! After a while my guide went straight on where I wanted to go right, up a slight hill to my house. I was now on my own.

It was very important that I slowed down and concentrated on the pavement and all the obstacles that were on it. Memory of my surroundings became top priority.

"Was there a lamp post coming up soon?" I kept thinking to myself.

Suddenly I stopped, thinking that I was about to get hit. I did this on several occasions, but was let off. No posts wanted to take me on and I was glad. Once again from memory, I had to work out how far along this road I lived. I stopped and turned to prepare myself to cross one more road, my last road! I stood and waited, and waited a little more. The traffic was passing me with great speed. I waited and listened for that gap, that silence. The only worries I had now were those silent ghosts on bikes.

"Here goes," I thought as I held my breath and prayed.

I crossed hesitantly and reached the pavement on the other side. With a large step I was now safe.

"Thank you God," I repeated several times.

As I walked along looking for my home I noticed that most of the houses had no gates.

"This house looks like mine, I think!"

I felt around with my hands until they stumbled on what felt like a gate.

"Now to open it, where's the lever, and which side is it on?"

Eventually I found it and entered my garden.

"Where's the door handle?" I thought as I struggled to find it.

Eventually my hand stumbled on the handle and I entered my home.

Distressed from my whole ordeal, I went to my bedroom. As I lay there on my bed I struggled to stop the vivid thoughts rushing through my mind.

"Am I going to go blind? Is this how some visually impaired people have to see?"

The thoughts continued as I began to cry, tears streaming down my face as I worried about my future.

"I'm going to be an invalid, disabled for the rest of my life."

I lay there that awful depressing night and I cried and cried until I finally fell asleep.

CHAPTER 3

The Art of guessing

The next morning I opened my eyes to see more blurred images around the room. Nothing was in focus.

"What am I going to do, will I ever see again?" I thought hysterically.

I sat there for a moment almost bursting into tears and feeling sorry for myself. Then it hit me. I suddenly realised that I hadn't put my glasses on yet. My heart began to race again and I became excited. I placed them on my face and the world became clear again.

"I can see!" I shouted ecstatically.

The smile came back to my face as I looked through my glasses and felt blessed by having the privilege of being able to see. The difference was incredible. Plain blue curtains turned out to have pretty little patterns on them with a mosaic of colours. The difference that my glasses made was incredible, so I removed them and then replaced them once more to see the amazing transformation again.

"I'm back," I mumbled.

It felt wonderful to be able to see again. I felt lucky and started to appreciate having this precious gift.

I decided to talk to my parents about our family history. My mother said that she had no recollection of anyone in her family going blind. My dad surprised me and said that one of his brothers had gone blind when he was quite young and had then suddenly died. I was now curious about why and how he had died suddenly. My father was a positive man and started to give me some advice.

"Don't worry about your eyes," he said. "You won't go blind."

I listened some more.

"God will open your eyes and you will see people more clearly," my dad said.

"How can I see more clearly if my eyesight is going to get worse?" I asked, wondering what he meant.

"Don't worry, you will see," he replied.

We spoke for a short while longer then I left.

The next day I went to work. I worked in a local school as a Computer Technician. This involved assisting both students and teachers with all their computer needs. I managed to use the standard keyboards and 14-inch screens. When students needed help I would go to them and look at their screen, then sometimes talked them through the step-by-step procedures or corrected whatever the problem was for them. Sometimes they had produced colourful drawings and just wanted the yellow section to be moved so I would assist them. Working with the teachers was always a highlight of my day because it felt like I was teaching the teachers and that always made me feel extra special. The students were easier to teach because the teachers panicked like big babies! One of the teachers who I often helped used to teach me at my old high school. Imagine how good it felt to tell someone off who used to tell me off ten years earlier!

At lunchtime we had fun. It became a major part of the students' day because I used to put on a few games and pupils loved to play and let their hair down. They loved it so much that most of them showed me great respect only because they knew that I could ban them from using the games or computer room at any time. We did give priority to any students wanting to do serious coursework because that was more important than playing games!

I had a few favourite students who would always come at lunchtime to see me even if they hadn't reserved a computer. Some of them started training with me and after more that fifteen years they still train. Other students used to offer to get my lunch, but I soon found out that they were enjoying my lunch too! My favourite student was Tanya. She used to buy me two sausage rolls and come back with one. The other one would be in her tummy. Other times I would leave a sandwich on my desk while I went to help another pupil. When I got back I would notice that there was a bite taken out of it. I knew that it was her because food only disappeared when she was around. She added fun to lunchtimes but at a cost – my food!

Even my boss was great and you can't say that about many bosses. She trusted me and gave me a lot of power to change things whenever I thought that they needed changing.

The end of my working day seemed to come quickly. I was kept busy and the days just flew by.

About three times a week I headed to the Rugby Leisure Centre for my regular Martial Arts training. I'd been doing Martial Arts for five years and I trained about three times a week at this local class. I pursued several different sports and hobbies, including weight training and roller-skating, but Martial Arts was my favourite. I practised a lot at home, where I would train at least five times a week for about an hour each time. My life revolved around my training to which I gave serious dedication. During this period I was training to become a black belt and I was just one belt away from achieving that.

After the warm-up was over my instructor asked me to take part of the class. This was standard procedure when you get to my level so by now I felt comfortable teaching them. My progression from the beginners row at the back of the class to the front row, right next to the black belts seemed quite quick, and there I was, teaching. After about half an hour my instructor relieved me from my duty and said that it was now my turn to be taught.

In just a few weeks I would be taking my black belt grading exam and my instructor wanted to go through a few important sections that he thought I needed to improve. Although I felt confident, I trusted the experience of my instructor. The first section was self-defence. He told me that my timing was slightly slow when I took my glasses off. After explaining my difficulty focussing without my glasses and that I had recently been registered as partially sighted, he told me to work even harder to perfect the skill of being able to recognise unfocused images quickly and accurately. The way that I conquered my problems was by guessing. If I thought that someone had a knife in their hand, I would assume that it was quite long and block accordingly. When my instructor was happy he moved me onto the next section, which was breaking boards.

My timing was slightly off due to my blurred vision so once again I worked extremely hard at guessing. The techniques that I struggled with the most were the ones that involved me turning around before kicking.

Once the lesson was over the instructor asked the people who were going to take their black belts to stay behind for some extra tuition. Over the previous few months he had been concentrating on a great deal of breaking techniques using our hands. We were about to find out why he had been so determined to toughen up our hands. He pulled several bricks out of his bag of tricks. They were real house bricks. He got down on his knees and started to set them up; one brick on its side on the left and one on the right with another one suspended in the middle like a bridge. This last brick had the flat part on top. He measured a few times while concentrating very hard. His arm slowly touched the brick and then he brought it right up high into the air only to repeat his actions. When he was confident he swung his arm high and then in a fast swoop chopped the brick with the outside of his hand between his little finger and wrist. The brick smashed in two and then he said; "And now it's your turn."

One by one we took turns at smashing the brick. There were five of us being assessed and I was the third one to have a go. They all took several attempts but eventually they broke it to pieces. Then it was my turn.

The bricks were placed before me in a pile of mess. Trying to be smart I decided to use one of the side bricks from the previous person's attempt as the one that I would break. It had been crushed by the other bricks so I was hoping that it had been weakened. I knelt down and began to set the bricks up. When I had placed the bridge brick on top I began to slide the other two further apart. The bricks slid slightly too far apart and the bridge brick that I was going to break fell.

"How embarrassing," I muttered to myself.

"Concentrate and try again."

The bricks were set up again and I had put the other two bricks as far apart as I could without making the central one fall.

"The wider apart they are, the less power needed to break it," I thought as I sat there meditating.

The time had come to start measuring so I put my right hand onto the centre of the brick. Then I made sure that the knife-edge of my hand was on the brick as though I was going to chop it. At this point I curled my four fingers slightly and touched my thumb against them. This made my hand hard and firm enough so that when I finally did try to break the brick, my fingers wouldn't clash together, as that could quite easily cause my fingers to be damaged. With my hand on the brick I just sat there. It felt a little uncomfortable so I picked my left leg up and put the sole of my foot on the floor. This felt much more comfortable and it also felt like I could generate more power from this position.

"Take your time," my instructor hinted.

My hand was back on the brick and I proceeded to bring my right hand up high and then straight back down. My left hand was touching the brick to stop it from moving when I repeatedly touched it.

"Concentrate," I said to myself as I began breathing more heavily.

I had touched the brick several times now and I knew that it was time to break it. After placing my hand on the brick for the last time I paused… and then I brought my hand up high and down again to hit the brick with a thud. It had not broken and my hand began to tingle.

"I don't believe it," I thought in disappointment.

The brick had not broken and it was there, just staring at me.

"Well, I think I chose the wrong brick," I muttered.

"Would you like to try again?" my instructor asked.

"Sir!" I shouted as I checked the position of the bricks.

The bricks were set up and I prepared for my second strike.

"Is your hand hurting?" my instructor asked.

"Just a bit sir," I replied.

"Then break it this time and it won't hurt," suggested my instructor.

"I will break it this time sir," I cried in determination.

This time I swung my hand in a slight circular action like you would use to chop a tree with an axe. It felt a bit uncomfortable for a while, but then I got used to it. My concentration was back.

"Concentrate," I repeated several times.

"This feels good. You can do it, go for it!" I finally thought as I paused on the brick.

With an almighty thud and a shout I had hit the brick, but I didn't feel much pain. When I looked down the brick was lying in two. I had broken a brick for the first time and was now ready to take my black belt exam.

CHAPTER 4

Open your eyes

The time came for me to attend my next eye appointment and things were not looking good. I had already noticed that things that I had been able to see a few months before were now much less visible. People's faces were looking even more blurred. I struggled to see my opponents when taking my black belt grading exam. I didn't know to what extent my sight had changed, nor by how much it had deteriorated. This time I went prepared for bad news and took a friend along with me to guide me back home safely.

It wasn't long before I was called in for my first test.

"Can you cover your left eye and read that chart please?"

The moment had finally come for me to find out how much my eyes had deteriorated or whether they had miraculously cured themselves! I proceeded to read the big letter that was all on its own. Then I read the first line and felt somewhat relieved, I struggled with the second line and when I tried to decipher the third, I couldn't.

"I could read that line last time," I thought desperately.

It was obvious that my right eye was worse than it had been and I became slightly tearful, but I knew that my left eye had yet to be tested.

"Can you cover your right eye now please and read from the chart with your left?"

"Here we go," I thought to myself.

I did as I was instructed and covered my right eye. The large letter wasn't looking too clear and I began to have a bad feeling. As I struggled to read the first line I knew that there was no hope of me reading the second. I sat there despondently hoping that my eye would slowly get better and become clearer but I waited in vain. So I proceeded to guess the letters on the second line. I tried everything because I wasn't ready to accept the obvious. After making a dismal attempt I returned to my friend who was still sitting in the waiting room.

"I knew there was something wrong, I felt it," I thought to myself.

The next half an hour wait seemed interminable; it was as if someone had stopped time. I sat and had plenty of time to become sorry for myself.

"What's happening to me? Why does this have to happen to me? How bad are my eyes going to get?"

My eyes were getting worse and there was nothing I could do about it. My left eye was worse than my right and continuing to deteriorate at it's own pace.

"Maybe there's a cure," I thought as I was called in for my second test.

I followed the doctor and entered his room. As I sat on the chair I put my chin on the chin rest and peered at the white satellite dish that represented my field of vision. They had drawn up a graph with the results of my last test and would compare this to the new graph they would draw today. This would determine where the deteriorations were taking place. I had to press a button every time I saw the light. I remembered playing it like a game last time, but this time it felt like I was responding less, which set alarm bells ringing in my head.

My emotions began to trouble me and I felt that there was something seriously wrong.

"Are you pressing the button whenever you see the light?"

"I am. I can't see the light very often."

He continued to mark his sheet.

Watching carefully I noticed that I could see the light earlier from my left.

"Does this mean that I can see more clearly from the left?" I wondered.

After a few more minutes he moved the light around in my blind spots and although I could hear him moving his light around, I couldn't see it. Then I heard him joining all the dots together and shading in the parts where I couldn't see.

I put my glasses on and waited for him to complete his sketch.

"How bad is it?" I asked.

"It's quite good."

"Then why did you ask me if I was pressing the button?"

"There was quite a large area where you couldn't see and I was just checking."

"Has it changed much from the last time?"

"Your left eye is showing a significant increase in areas where you have no vision."

"Is it a lot?"

"The professor will go into more detail."

He led me back out to the waiting room. My body felt weak. I was drained and not looking forward to anything else. I wanted to go home and cry. Thoughts rushed through my mind and I felt like someone had just died. The fight to go on had almost disappeared. It was too much for me to accept so early on in my life. I felt tearful but there were too many people around for me to get hysterical. I didn't say much to my friend, no, I didn't want to talk about slowly losing my eyesight. I sat and looked at my surroundings, waiting for my next test, hoping that it wouldn't be much worse.

After ten minutes I was called into another room. I sat with my chin on another chin rest and a doctor asked me to remove my glasses. He then moved a blue lens on the machine closer to my eye, first my left then my right. After writing a few things down he looked at the back of my eyes with an ophthalmoscope.

"I need to put some eye drops in to dilate your eyes."

"Do you have to?" I pleaded.

"Yes, it's the only way we can get a good look at the back of your eyes."

I really hated having this done. These were the eye drops that had made me see people as ghosts and that was scary. Though very reluctant, I let him put the drops into my eyes and then he sent me back out for another twenty minutes to let them take effect. I sat and watched as the world slowly disappeared before my very eyes. The lights gradually became brighter and more distorted as my eyes started to dilate. As this happened they began to hurt more and more and I struggled to keep them open. The leaflets on the shelves looked like someone had poured water all over the words and they were starting to smudge. The magazines on the table had disappeared and the details on the photos were distorted as if they were melting. Someone appeared to have rubbed the letter off the large sign that said 'Desk A'. The person sitting opposite suddenly had one-tone clothes and she looked like she was wearing a mask over her face. Everything around me looked as if it had been thrown into a giant blender and mixed together until nothing was recognisable. My world was changing and I had to sit there until the transformation was complete. The group of people walking past were so blurred that they didn't appear to possess any limbs. They all looked like ghosts. It felt really uncomfortable looking at the ghostly figures before me, they began to scare me so I closed my eyes and thought, "The ghosts are back so the transformation must be complete."

My friend could tell that I wasn't feeling well. Maybe it was the tears dripping from my eyes that made it obvious. He went to the cafeteria and brought back a sandwich for me.

"Look at the world through my eyes," I thought, "it doesn't even look real, ghostly figures everywhere."

It was my turn to see the doctor and I entered the room once more. This time I had to link arms and be led into the room. The doctor looked at my eyes with a brilliantly bright light and it hurt. He held my eyelids open once more and told me to look straight ahead. My eyes kept trying to close but he wouldn't let them. Sometimes I looked away because of the sheer pain that the light was causing me. It felt like a massive torch being held against my eye or as if I was looking straight at the dazzling sun. My eyes were dilated and it made things appear larger.

"There's quite a lot of scarring here. Your disc is dark," he said as he continued his examination.

When he had finished he wrote down a few notes and asked me some questions.

"Have you noticed any pain in your eyes?"

"Yes, they seem to hurt quite a bit on a daily basis."

"The pressure in your eyes is a little high so I'll prescribe some eye drops to it bring down."

"What's causing the pressure?" I asked.

"You also have a condition called glaucoma."

"Oh great, I have RP and glaucoma?"

"Yes, but the eye drops will help to reduce the pressure."

"So what's next?"

"There's no need to do any more tests. We already know you have night blindness so you just have to see the professor for the results of your tests."

"Thanks, but I think that I already know my results."

CHAPTER 5

Let the fight begin

There were several adjustments to my lifestyle that was necessary in order to cope with my deteriorating eyesight. One of the biggest changes that I had to get used to was asking other people to read my letters. Most letters were fine but when they had to read some of my more private letters, I was embarrassed. They even asked questions about some of the letters they were reading and they found out whether I had money in my bank account. I felt useless having to ask and having to share my secrets. It was like my independence had been taken away from me.

Then one morning I woke up and noticed a difference. I got ready for work and went to catch the bus. Everywhere looked misty but it wasn't that cold.

"That's strange," I thought, "maybe my glasses are dirty."

Replacing my glasses after cleaning them made no difference so I tried once more. Everywhere still looked misty. It was a strange feeling that baffled me.

It was like fog. It wasn't thick but it was definitely visible and affecting my vision. Windows looked grey and were no longer completely transparent. The doors of houses, bricks, walls and gates seemed to have a cloudy finish to them. People's faces were slightly hazy. It felt like someone had turned down the contrast on a television so that all the colours were starting to blend in with each other. Cars began to blend in with the road as well. Something was wrong!

"It must be foggy. I've cleaned my glasses so I know it's not that."

As I walked past a lamp post it became more visible from the side. It was as though I could see more clearly from out of the sides of my eyes. From the front, the lamp post almost blended in with the sky and the pavement, everything had a grey haze to it. As I passed the lamp post it appeared to stand out more from the pavement and the other surroundings. It baffled me and I began to worry. My eyes darted around as if they were confused with where to look. Sometimes I would be looking straight on then found myself focussing on objects to the side of me. I kept switching from my left eye to my right and sometimes I could see double. I discovered that when I closed one eye I could see more clearly. When I looked at a passing car it seemed as if there were two vehicles very close to each other and when I tilted my head or closed one eye, it would become one car again. This began to scare me and I didn't know where to look.

"What's happening now? Why is that lamp post more visible from the side and why is everything slightly grey like fog? Is it foggy? Maybe I'm still half asleep but then why have I got double vision some of the time? I'll clean my eyes with water when I get to work."

By this time I had arrived at my bus stop. It's only a two-minute walk from my house, literally around the corner and there are no roads to cross. As I stood there for a second I observed the mist. A friend was also waiting at the bus stop.

"Good morning!"

"Morning and how are you?" he asked.

"I'm fine thanks but it's a little foggy today."

"Is it? It seems clear to me. It's cloudy but not foggy," he replied.

"Well it looks slightly foggy to me but my glasses probably need cleaning," I said jokingly.

I knew that my glasses were clean but until I found out what was happening, I thought that it was the easiest thing to blame.

While we waited for the bus I continued to wonder why I was seeing fog.

"Now I know that it isn't my glasses and I know that it's not really foggy. It must be my eyes. Maybe I still have some sleep in them and it's affecting my vision. I will definitely clean my face at work."

The bus had arrived at my work and I made my way in. After putting my bag down in my room, I switched all the computers on and went to wipe my eyes in the washroom. I washed away the sleep from my eyes and replaced my glasses. Although the difference was very slight, it had helped but everything still seemed a little foggy.

"Now I know that it's not real fog because it's still slightly foggy in here," I thought to myself. "But there can't be any sleep in my eyes because I've just washed them."

Then I went to look at my reflection in the mirror.

"Where have my glasses gone and why does my face look grey? If my eyes are worse, then why the fog?"

I returned to my duties.

I then discovered that my keyboard was very difficult to read. I experienced the same problems with reading words on the computer screen.

"It's my eyes isn't it? They've become worse. I can't believe this. It's my job as a computer technician to type and read screens. If I can no longer do this how will I cope? Everything appears to be more distorted."

It frustrated me as I tried to focus.

Over the past year I had learned to cope with my visual impairment, I had adjusted my life to cope with the changes to my eyesight. I was writing less frequently, reading with books much closer to my face, I'd had to give up roller-skating and had changed my teaching methods. Now it appeared that my sight had decided to deteriorate further which would require even more changes. My anger grew as I thought about how I would cope with the changes to my eyesight.

I told my boss about the problems that I was experiencing and she helped as much as she could. She assigned me two prefects who helped with some of the jobs that I was struggling with.

Nobody knew how much I was frustrated by not being able to do my job as well as I used to. Sometimes my every thought would be about my disability and I would continually try to fight the thoughts and erase them from my head. Hatred and anger were ripe in my mind. I would often become angry from not being able to perform well and would sometimes get aggressive towards others for not understanding after I had told them about my problems. Being aggressive was my way of coping, an outlet for my frustrations. I didn't mean to be like that, I just had to or I could see myself becoming more and more depressed. My mind was full of thoughts that hurt to think about and I desperately needed to find ways of stopping them from taking over my head and my life.

When helping during classes I experienced some more problems. A problem that I experienced was with colours. Many students would draw objects in different colours then want to move some of them. Sometimes they couldn't get the program to do what they wanted and they would ask me for help. Yellow appeared white to me and it didn't matter how hard I looked it stayed invisible. Every time I encountered a new difficulty it would add to my anger and would sometimes prevent me from finding solutions.

Computer cables also became a challenge because I could no longer see where to plug wires in, but after memorising where everything connected, I was able to rewire a whole room full of computers, printers and control boxes literally by touch alone. I would place a finger behind the computer and run it along the back. After feeling where all the sockets were I would then guide the cables in. Being able to turn the computer around wouldn't help much because everything appeared blurred. My lack of clear vision was causing problems throughout my working day and although I really enjoyed my job I was sometimes grateful to reach the end of my working day.

One day on the way home I went to see my mother as usual; my sisters were there and it was obvious that they weren't feeling too happy. Three of them had been to the Birmingham Eye Hospital for tests; my brothers were still reluctant to go as they were worried about the possibility of receiving bad news and I didn't blame them. It's a crushing blow to be told that you may go blind and that it could happen at any time. They were not prepared to accept the possibility and so avoided going. They wanted to enjoy their lives as much as possible by acting as though nothing was wrong with their eyes.

However, my sisters were curious. Angela, Carline and June had gone along to be tested and had their results. Jennifer had some problems and was short-sighted. I felt that she should have gone too but she was reluctant like my brothers and didn't want to know, she wanted to carry on with her life. All three of my sisters who had been to the hospital were suffering the after effects of the eye drops that had been used to dilate their eyes. Two of my sisters were blessed, it had been confirmed that they didn't have RP, but their relief and joy was overpowered by the fact that Angela had been diagnosed with the condition. She was very upset. She had gone to her appointment thinking that she was just short-sighted but had wanted the doctors to examine her eyes in the hope that it would provide them with more knowledge that might help my brother and me.

Some of her words rang bells in my memory – they were the same words that I had used not so long ago. She had known that she was just short-sighted, but deep down she had also known that something else wasn't quite right. When she was younger her eyesight had been so good that she had taken some driving lessons. She is ten years older than me and has experienced the changes much later on in her life than I did. Angela was very distraught from the news and felt like her life was over. After watching our brother suddenly become blind she knew the dangers that may be upon her at any time. She now had the same worries as me, like waking up one day blind.

CHAPTER 6

Suffering in silence

At my next appointment I was already expecting bad news. It wasn't clear to me how much my eyes had deteriorated further but it was obvious that there had been a change.

The first test was over and my result was already clear. My right eye had gone from reading two lines down, to just one and was now seeing what my left had a year ago. It was frustrating to hear and to know, but there was nothing I could do about it.

My left eye had gone from reading just one line to a dismal amount that wasn't worth seeing. The first time I had my eyes tested at the Eye Hospital I thought that the solitary big letter was huge and pathetically easy to read, so big that anyone should be able to read it with their glasses on, yet that was all I could now see with my left eye. That was all I could read and even then it wasn't very clear. It looked distorted. It was vaguely ridiculous to think about and I had trouble accepting it. I was only a few years into my tests and was just about able to read the top letter, but it was only just legible. The letter was slightly out of focus and I was able to determine it by guessing.

"How bad are my eyes? Can't they just stay the same now? How much worse are they going to become?"

The thoughts worried and distressed me as I fought to keep them out of my mind.

The next test was the satellite dish to determine my field of vision. My patience was wearing thin as I progressed through to the end. The parts of my eyes on which I had blind spots were growing rapidly. They were beginning to take over my eyes and were also affecting my central vision, which is why I was appearing to see some objects better from out of the sides of my eyes. The doctor asked several times if I was pressing the button whenever I saw the light. The more he asked the clearer it became that my eyesight was failing and the angrier I became.

The next doctor tested the pressure of my eyes and looked into the back of them with his ophthalmoscope. He put the wonderful eye drops in. This was always the highlight of my appointment because my eyesight was already grossly distorted, but with the addition of the eye drops things became even more blurred.

After the test the doctor said that there was more pressure in my eyes. The fight in my head started once more.

"Am I supposed to sit here and just take it?"

"There's nothing you can do about it so accept it," a conflicting voice replied.

"It's not that easy to accept that you are disabled. Why is this happening to me?"

The anger and rage took over me once more.

The doctor referred me to the professor for the rest of my diagnosis and as usual the professor took a few moments while he studied my results.

"Your eyes appear to have deteriorated even further. The tests show that your left eye is almost unable to read from the chart and slowing down when reacting to movement. Both your eyes are showing signs of tunnel vision."

All I could do was sit there and listen to someone pronouncing my sentence. One after another he stated my problems as he continued to rip my life to shreds.

"Can I look into your eyes and see your discs again?"

"Help yourself. It won't make any difference to me."

"I understand how you feel, but it will help you in the long run. It will help us to know more about RP and speed up the process of finding a cure. Most doctors don't even know what it looks like so would be fascinated to look into your eyes."

He took a good look into my eyes and then wrote down a few notes.

"The discs in your eyes are showing more signs of damage. Are you having many more problems getting around?"

It was my turn to talk and I unloaded some of my thoughts onto him.

"My whole life has changed. It's like it's no longer in my hands. I just have to accept whatever happens. I've had to give up roller-skating because it's done mostly in poor light and I'm really struggling in the dark at the moment. Everything also looks more distorted so that's affecting my job and general lifestyle."

"In what way?" he asked.

"Well I can no longer read barcodes. The text on the computer screen has to be much bigger. I work with software companies that design their installation sequence in small text. Sometimes I have to take my glasses off to read it and my face is literally touching the screen. The keyboard is nearly impossible to read. If I didn't know where the keys were I probably wouldn't be able to continue my job."

"You're experiencing quite a few problems then?"

"That's nothing. It's affecting me throughout the day, every day now. I'm struggling to find my toothbrush. Most of my clothes look the same colour and sometimes I put my shirts on inside out because of my lack of sight. I can no longer see myself in the mirror; I look like I'm wearing a mask. When I shave I can't see my hairs, I just guess. Now I can't see dirt and keep worrying that things are dirty. I'm struggling walking around. Sometimes I bump into things and I'm terrified when crossing the road. I have to ask for help when I'm in a shop because I can hardly see or read labels. I have to guess people's names because I can't see them clearly."

"Is there anything else?" he asked.

"I wake up every morning not knowing whether I'll be able to see. Everywhere looks so distorted that my sight is cloudy. I can hardly read a book any more and it makes me feel so jealous seeing other people reading. My writing is getting worse and I can no longer use cashpoint machines. It's not worth me watching television these days because the picture is so distorted that it hurts my eyes to look at it. Sometimes I have to ask other people to read my letters. Do you realise how humiliated that makes me feel?"

"I wish I could do more to help. We've had your sister's results and I have to admit that we're confused. She wasn't supposed to have RP. She should have been a carrier. We will need blood tests. Oh, and we're moving to new premises, so we'll send you the details."

"My sister wasn't supposed to have RP and we're not supposed to have hearing difficulties? What's going on?"

I became angry and confused. Here I was with a specialist who had performed numerous tests and was still unsure of the nature of my disabilities.

"Let's wait for the results of the blood tests, and then we'll know. Have your parents said any more about their family history?"

"My mother said that nobody suffered blindness and my father passed away recently, and there was so much that I wanted to ask him."

"I'm sorry to hear that. Have you seen a counsellor yet?"

"I'm fine. I don't need one. I just need a new pair of eyes."

"Have any blind associations been in touch yet?"

"No; why?"

"They'll provide you with some help with getting around. I'll contact them again."

The conversation came to an end and I made my way home with my friend.

CHAPTER 7

Living with my disability

At long last help was on the way. In 1993 I received a phone call from an association to assist me with my disability. They were sending over an assistant to give me more information on how to cope with my visual impairment.

A young lady turned up at my house at the prearranged time. Her name was Rita and she worked for the Warwickshire Association for the Blind (WAB).

"We received information that you're in need of assistance. I need to know how much vision you have left and if you are in need of some specialist equipment at work."

It felt uncomfortable talking about it, but I was in for a surprise.

"Well as usual they're difficult questions to answer. Although I can see, my vision is so poor that I'm registered as partially sighted. I can see the picture on the television, but not in great detail. Most of my friends know that I'm partially sighted but I still feel uncomfortable sharing it with others."

"Well, I want you to try and relax while you're telling me about your eyes and the problems that you've incurred. I know that it's difficult to open up and share your thoughts, but it will help. I must admit that… I'm registered blind!"

This came as a shock to me and I felt a weird sensation.

"How can she help me if she can't see?" I thought to myself.

She had come with a helper so I assumed that he would do her work.

"You're blind?"

"Yes," she said. "So I understand exactly how you feel. Now tell me more about your problems."

"I can't see the video below my television any more and my hi-fi is a dark blob to me so I have trouble using them both."

"That's because your eyesight is darker than you realise."

She seemed to understand what I was trying to say and it soon made me feel comfortable enough to share some more thoughts.

"Tell me more about your mobility problems."

"Well I'm used to having my independence and going out quite a lot but as my eyesight is deteriorating I don't feel like venturing out so much. I never realised how much I depended on my eyes until now. Nearly everything involves sight. Seeing people, reading and writing, watching television, using a computer, finding things that have dropped, cooking, going shopping and crossing the road. There's too much to mention."

I became heated as I brushed my hands through my hair through sheer frustration.

"I don't want to be blind. Why is this happening to me? What have I done to deserve this? It really makes me angry when I can't do something simple that I would be able to do if I could see."

The anger and frustration built up as I shared my inner thoughts.

"Are you seeing a counsellor?"

"No; I don't need anyone, I'm fine."

"It's time to face what could happen. You will need to learn Braille and also learn how to get around using a white cane."

"Me! Using a white cane?"

It made me nervous. There was me, trying my hardest to cope with my visual impairment but I had never pictured myself using a white stick. I began to feel distressed and dizzy.

"It's up to you. Would you like to learn how to use one? I can teach you."

I hesitated.

"Are my eyes going to get so bad that I have to use a white stick?" I asked.

"Probably; I do think that it's best if you learn, just in case."

"But they're long and... I might as well wear a t-shirt that says, 'I'm blind'. It's degrading; I can't, I can't!"

"You can carry it folded up until you feel comfortable using it."

I paused to think again.

"What do you mean, that you will teach me? Can't I just have the stick?" I asked.

"No, there's a technique to using a white cane, I'll teach you."

"You're going to teach me? You're not going to ask someone else to teach me?"

"I can use one, I'm blind, remember?" she replied jokingly.

"Exactly; it would be like the blind... leading the blind. Now this I have to see!"

The thought of how Rita would be able to guide me when I could see more than she could fascinated me. We arranged to meet in a week and I eagerly awaited her return.

The week passed quickly and it was soon time for my lesson. Rita walked in with her helper and sat down. She took out my new toy – my white cane. It was folded up small, so she showed me how to unravel it and it became quite long and slim.

"Are you ready for your first lesson?"

"Yes, where are we going to practise walking?"

"We'll start on a road that's already familiar to you. I've taught a few other people there as well so I'm used to it."

She told me that it was Hillmorton Road, outside the Sports Centre that I used regularly and then we set out on our way.

Her driver drove us there. He never helped much; he just did the driving. She literally did everything herself. He stopped outside the park and we got out. She arranged to meet him back in the same place in an hour and we stood on the pavement as he drove off.

"Open your cane first," she instructed.

I unfolded it and the short sections interlocked with each other and my stick was straight and ready to be used. It was about five foot long and very slim.

"I'm ready," I said.

She linked my right arm and off we went. She began to talk to me and I had a little trouble hearing her. I wasn't going to say anything because I thought that she'd think that I was only fit for the bin, being deaf and partially sighted, but she sounded too muffled.

"I'm sorry if I didn't mention this, but I'm deaf in my right ear so I can hardly hear you on that side."

"That's fine, can you hear anything?"

"No; my right ear is totally deaf and so I usually have people on my left side. My left ear picks up what you're saying but it sounds muffled as if you were talking to me while I'm under the water in a swimming pool."

We stopped and she swapped sides.

"This makes a difference in the type of white cane that you need."

"In what way?" I asked curiously.

"White canes are for blind people, but if you also have a hearing deficiency then your cane will be white with red stripes."

"Wow! I didn't know that. I thought that all white canes were the same."

"No, they're not, we'll order you a new cane. Now let me show you how to use it."

We stood there for a moment while she opened her white cane too.

"Put your cane down to touch the pavement, now move it to your right. Then take a step closer to it with your right foot. Now move your cane to your left where you would walk with your left foot. Now take a step forward with your left foot."

"Like this?" I asked, having a go.

Through My Eyes

"No, try again like this," she demonstrated.

"That feels awkward, why can't I just hold the stick in front of me and walk?"

"Because your feet don't take the same path. Doing it that way you might still bump into things with your body. The way that I'm teaching you makes your cane search out the path of each of your feet just before you take a step."

I followed her instructions and off we went, walking cautiously forward, both using our white canes.

We walked along, tapping our sticks on the pavement and then stepping forwards.

"Slow down, we're coming to the road. Right, stop here and we'll turn around and walk back," she said.

"This isn't as bad as I thought it would be."

"You get used to it."

"I'm not too keen on touching it on the floor though," I stated.

"Why?"

"Well, I'm always worried that I'm going to walk in dog muck and now I'm worried that my stick will touch some and… it's disgusting. I hate it! I'm always worried that I've stepped in some and the more obsessive I'm becoming the more I can smell it."

"That's disgusting!" she answered laughingly.

She laughed at my obsession as we walked on.

"Let's take this path to the Sports Centre," she said.

"How did you know that was there, I thought that you couldn't see?"

"I've been here many times but most importantly, I try to memorise my surroundings wherever I go."

"You too? I thought that I was the only one who did that but now that I think about it, that's how most visually impaired people probably get around. It hurts me though."

"What do you mean?" she asked.

"Having to think of everything while I walk, it gives me a headache. It's usually after a hard day's thinking that my eyes hurt more too and it's really uncomfortable. The pressure is so great I have to take my glasses off and rub my eyes."

"Get used to it. You need to know when a lamp post is coming up before you get to it."

"It's too much to think about. Sometimes I feel like my head is going to explode. Everywhere I go I remember things that most people can just look and see when they need to. I know that there are two benches on the left of this path and at the end of the path it dips slightly before the opening in the fence on the left. It's almost unnecessary information but it stops me from walking into the locked gate that's straight ahead."

"You need to keep doing it, memorising everything because as your eyesight gets worse that's all you'll have to help you manoeuvre around objects."

"I will."

Just then I felt my foot slip.

"What was that?" I asked.

"What's wrong?" she replied.

"My foot just slid on something. Now I'll never know whether it was mud or dog muck. I can't see well enough to look at my shoes and… I feel sick."

"Here comes that gate. Let's stop and have a rest then we'll walk back."

We rested for a few minutes, exchanging thoughts. It was so soothing to find someone who really understood my thoughts. She had the same thoughts and feelings as me. She experienced troubled times and moments where she too felt useless. My confidence grew and we continued to chat.

"Sometimes I feel so useless and incompetent having to ask others for help all the time," I said. "People tell me that I should ask for help more often, but when I do, sometimes they're not able to help and then I feel incapable of doing things for myself. I feel like a burden to others and end up trying to do things for myself. Sometimes that's okay because if feels like I'm gaining some of my independence back. I hate going to parties where you have to help yourself to food. It all looks like merged clumps of blurred paint to me, and nothing's identifiable. Then I have to stand there with my plate while others tell me what's on the table. Most of the time, they then have to serve me. I feel like a baby, not being able to do things for myself."

"If you carry this white cane then people will understand," she advised.

"But I don't want to be labelled, I don't want to be partially sighted, I want to be normal again. I want to be able to do things for myself."

"How did you feel using the cane?"

"It was fun, a little embarrassing, especially when we were passing people. Imagine what they must be thinking seeing two people with white sticks walking together. A pair of misfits, that's what we probably looked like."

"Do you remember your surroundings from where we walked from?"

"Most of it, I think, why?" I asked innocently.

"We're going to walk back but this time I want you to wear these."

She produced a pair of sunglasses.

"Put these on."

My glasses were too big and I couldn't get the dark glasses over them.

"They won't fit."

"That's fine; take your glasses off first."

"But I can't see without my glasses."

"Exactly; you need to get used to this feeling just in case your eyesight gets any worse."

So I removed my glasses and put the dark ones on. They were special sunglasses, very dark, big and bulky and oddly shaped. They also had an added surprise.

"I can't see anything through these, nothing," I said desperately.

"Move them around until you can see through the little pinholes."

"Pinholes? Where?"

"There's a small hole in each lens that allows you to see through. It blocks out most of the light that can irritate your eyes. It also imitates what tunnel vision can end up looking like."

It made me feel very uncomfortable and disorientated. The view was so dark and so blurred it was as though I was looking through a tunnel and only seeing the faint light at the other end. There was someone approaching, I could hear them so I looked around, trying to line my eyes up with the pinholes and focus on the movement. I saw a vague line in the distance that slowly became wider. It grew as the person got closer but it never became clearer. It was so cloudy looking and so distorted that it looked like a very faint ghostly apparition. As the shape passed me I almost trembled. It was so uncomfortable and scary to see like this.

"No way would I come out of my house and walk around if I saw like this, no way," I thought to myself frantically.

I readjusted the dark glasses until I could see, (well, see something) and we walked on. I was nervous, this felt very different. I couldn't see the trees or the lamp posts or even the path. I was very wary of each step that I took. I walked much slower too. My white stick detected me veering off the path onto the grass so I straightened up. It was so hard to control my balance as I became disorientated. We continued to retrace our path cautiously.

"How do you feel with those glasses on?" Rita asked.

"Very uncomfortable, I can't see anything and with being deaf in one ear, I feel dizzy and keep feeling like I'm going to fall over. It's an awful feeling and I don't know where I am or how far it is until we reach the end of this path."

"This is where your memory comes into play, trust yourself."

"We're walking slower so my timing is out too. I would say that we're close now."

I carried on walking and using my stick like it would save my life. We slowed down as I prepared to hit the gate with my stick. After a few more moments the stick made contact and I searched around with it as I shuffled to my right to find the opening. It was awkward but somehow I managed it.

"I did it!" I shouted joyfully.

"Well done. Now let's walk to our left."

We set off and plodded slowly along. We were near the road this time and the sound of the cars frightened me. I could see thin blurred strips, which were presumably people and they moved in a jerky fashion. They were unsure of where to walk and dodged us at the last second. Then my stick hit something. It was a post that I had forgotten was there.

"That was scary. For a second or two I didn't know what it was and panicked," I said.

After manoeuvring around the post I continued to lead her forward staying in the middle of the pavement by guessing how far away the road was from my right.

"Slow down we're coming to a road again. Remember, we'll turn around and walk back again," she said.

"Why don't we keep walking and cross the road?"

"You're not ready, not with those dark glasses on anyway. We'll cross roads on another lesson."

"Another lesson! I have to do this again?" I cried out.

"Yes, next week I'll teach you techniques on how to walk up and down steps and then we'll cross roads the week after."

As we walked on my stick sunk down as it hit the road at the edge of the pavement. We stopped, turned and walked back.

"We'll walk back to the park gate and then rest while we wait for our lift back to your house."

Halfway along, I suddenly stopped as I remembered that there was a post around somewhere. I slowed down all the way past the post and to the gate. After we arrived at the gate she asked me to remove my dark glasses. Although my sight was still distorted, I felt relieved to be able to see more light.

"Did you enjoy your first lesson?" she asked.

"It was fun but at the same time I felt helpless, terrified and very vulnerable. I struggle to see anyway but that was different. I felt like people were watching me and I didn't like the attention the stick drew. I enjoyed it, but I didn't, does that make any sense?" I replied in confusion.

"Yes... I think," she replied as she laughed.

"I'm scared," I said.

"Scared of what?"

"I'm scared of going blind and seeing like that. People think that I'm strong and brave to have carried on going out but I don't know if I can do it if my eyesight deteriorates much further. I really am scared of going blind."

"It is scary but we learn to cope, we have to," Rita replied.

We spoke for a few more minutes before a car drew up in front of us and beeped its horn.

"That sounds like our lift," Rita said.

"Wouldn't it be funny if we got into the wrong car?" I said jokingly.

We laughed and nervously got into the car.

CHAPTER 8

Through my eyes

An appointment had been organised for me to learn how to read Braille. At the allotted time, a young lady arrived at my home. She sat down and introduced herself. She amazed me just like Rita had, because she was full of life and energy but was registered blind. It encouraged me to know that there were people suffering more than I was who appeared positive and happy. It didn't matter how much I was suffering inside, I knew that I would feel much worse if I was registered blind.

She asked me how I managed to read.

"I have to read very slowly. Most words are too small to read and the ones that I do manage to read have parts missing. My eyes have blind spots that are growing and slowly taking over my vision. Depending on the size of the text, parts are missing. If it's larger then less appears to be missing, but most large words have a part of the corner missing as though someone has bitten a chunk out of it. It's so difficult that I hardly read any more."

"Would you like to learn Braille? Lots of books are available in Braille and you could start reading again."

"That would be great. I'd really appreciate it if you could teach me so that I can read books again. I'm really jealous of other people when I hear them read and wish that I could do it again too."

Then the lady took a book out of her bag and passed it over to me. It was a book written in Braille.

"There's nothing in this book, where's all the writing?" I asked jokingly.

"It's Braille. Can you feel the different textures?"

I ran my fingers over some of the pages and found it difficult to feel the difference.

"Sorry, but it feels almost smooth like there's nothing there."

She asked me to hand the book back and then passed me another one.

"This book is to practise Braille. Are you ready?"

"I was born ready," I chuckled.

"Can you feel the big bump with any of your fingers?"

It took a while but eventually I was able to feel something.

"How many dots are there?" she asked.

"I'm not sure; it's hard to tell; I would guess that there's just one."

"Well done."

"I can read Braille!" I bellowed.

"That's just one. How many can you feel on the next one?"

Moving my index finger carefully and softly, I felt around for a while. It was difficult and although I could feel something, I couldn't feel the separations so I guessed.

"There are two this time."

"No; try again and take your time."

"Are there three?"

"Yes, that's right."

"Sorry, but I just guessed that," I admitted.

"Don't guess; feel; try the next one."

It was so difficult. I tried for ages but couldn't feel anything significant.

"I'm really struggling; I think you must need really sensitive fingers to read Braille."

"You do; I'd have thought that you would have sensitive fingers from working with computers."

"Sorry, but didn't I tell you about my Martial Arts?"

Through My Eyes

I explained that I did lots of press-ups and broke bricks and boards with my hands. She was disappointed and held my hands to see how soft they were.

"My fingers are too rough and not as sensitive as I thought. It would be asking too much for me to give up my Martial Arts to be able to read Braille. It's too hard and I don't think that I'm going to be able to do it."

My fingers had lost their sensitivity and I struggled to read anything.

"I'm sorry but you really are having a great deal of trouble."

"I might as well give up now before I become emotionally attached. It would only make me feel like more of a failure if I persisted and was still unable to identify the dots."

"Don't worry; only about 10% of blind people are able to read Braille."

I'll never know if she was telling the truth or just trying to make me feel better, which was probably for the best. My dream of reading a book was left as a dream and I had to learn to accept the fact that reading a book was a thing of the past.

Some more people came to see me regarding specialist equipment. This time two people turned up at my place of work. We had arranged for them to come at a time when my room was empty for a while. We discussed my needs for a while and then they went to fetch what equipment they thought would be required. Then they set it all up as I sat and watched. I noticed how easy they made it look, the way they would look at something and then connect it in its correct place. I could tell that they were using their eyes a great deal and I almost became jealous. Once the equipment was ready they switched everything on and began explaining what they had brought.

"Look at that keyboard. It's exactly the same as yours but it has very large letters on the keys. Can you see the letters now?"

"Yes I can see. Wow! This is amazing."

The keyboard had a dark background instead of the standard grey and the letters were white, which made them stand out and much easier for me to see.

"Try using it. Does it help?"

"Yes, it really does make a big difference."

"There may be days that are slightly darker than others so beside your computer is a bright light – try it."

I switched on the light and everything stood out more clearly.

"I can't believe this! It's brilliant! Thank you very much."

For the first time in a long while joy surged through me.

"That's not all, there's more. Are you ready?"

"Yes," I said in anticipation.

"Look at your computer screen. Now type something small so that you struggle to see it."

I wrote a few sentences in a word processing program then waited.

"Is that hard to read?"

"It's very hard to read."

"OK, now press the control key and the plus key."

When I pressed the keys I nearly fell off my seat with amazement. My whole screen had magically enlarged. The words were bigger and the mouse pointer was bigger too.

"This is amazing!"

"Press the same keys a few times and then press the control and minus key, that will make everything on your computer screen smaller again."

Every time I pressed the keys everything on my screen grew. It went to a ridiculous size where I could only see a few letters on the screen at a time. As I moved my mouse pointer over to the word 'File' at the top left hand corner of my screen, it took up my entire screen. The magnifying package could grow to any size and then shrink back down when I pressed the control and minus keys. As I typed I could see that everything was clear and it followed everywhere I typed. Every time I moved the mouse the screen magnified where the cursor hovered and it also magnified where I typed. It was an ingeniously useful package. I felt comfortable on the magnifying level four times my usual screen size.

They then asked me to look at another monitor, which had a much bigger screen than usual.

"Do you think that this will help too?"

"A larger computer screen, yes please! That's a great help!"

"And here's a small torch for when you're in those hard to reach places."

The amount of equipment they had overwhelmed me. I was ecstatic. My boss had come into the room and was listening and watching intently. She was interested in purchasing some of the equipment for me. I was very grateful because I knew that not many bosses would have been so keen to buy equipment to assist a disabled person.

The final piece of equipment was by far the best.

"This is a CCTV, have you seen one before?"

"Yes, it's a camera for seeing people in shops and around town centres."

"This isn't the same. This is a special magnifier that enlarges the words in a book to almost any size."

"Book Reader… I can read books with it?" I asked excitedly.

"Yes; would you like to try it?"

"Of course I would!"

"Get one of the computer manuals that you struggle to read and put it under the bright light."

It was one of the most exciting things that I had seen in a very long time. There was a tray under the computer screen on which to place books. Then a bright light and a magnifying glass shone the book onto the computer screen. It had some buttons on the front of the CCTV to adjust the size of the writing similar to the magnifying package on my computer. At long last, after many failed attempts and only after sheer determination, I was now able to read books.

Having the ability to read restored upon me once more, I refrained from wasting any time. My brother advised me to read self help books because he thought that they would help me to see a positive side to life. He was right. The books I read changed my life in a positive way forever.

CHAPTER 9

You are blessed

My second child was born on the 9th of November 1994. Her mane is Jasmine, and like Michaela she too keeps me happy. Unfortunately my happiness was cut short when my mother passed away within months of the birth of Jasmine.

Although the loss of my parents was still quite fresh in my mind, I kept myself busy and tried not to dwell on the pain. It was as though someone was testing me, seeing how many challenges it would take to push me over the edge. Every time I learnt how to cope with the stresses in my life, along came another challenge to test me. The memories of my parents were still in my mind, but I was able to remain a positive person and seemed to get on with life.

There were other things on my mind now. It was only a few months after the death of my mother and it was time for my next eye appointment. It was at the new Eye Hospital and was very difficult to find but as usual I took a friend along to help me. We drove to Birmingham this time instead of travelling by train. We arrived and I registered with reception. All I had to do now was wait.

It took ages before I was called for my first test and in that time I began to get nervous.

Through My Eyes

I followed the doctor into the room and took a seat. The doctor told me to cover my left eye and to start reading from the chart.

"This is a joke!" I thought. "The letters look more blurred than ever, maybe my glasses are dirty or maybe my eyes are cloudier today."

After cleaning my glasses and blinking quite vigorously to clear my vision, I proceeded to read from the chart.

"The first letter is… A."

"Yes; go on."

"Are you sure that the chart isn't too far away?"

"No, it's not, why?"

"Well… that's all I can read. I can only see the first letter, all the rest look too blurred and distorted to identify."

"Are you sure? Can't you see any of the next line?"

I took a good, long, hard look.

"No; that's it. That's all I can read."

"Can you try and guess any of the letters on the next line?"

"They all look too distorted, I'm sorry but I can't."

My heart began to beat faster as I became more nervous. After a few seconds of entering the room I was already aware of the rate of deterioration in my right eye and I felt extremely uncomfortable.

"Would you like to try again using these dark glasses with pinholes?"

They passed me a pair of dark glasses similar to those I had used when I was learning to walk with a white cane. They had small holes in the lenses to help me focus on specific objects. It gave a tunnel vision effect so everything else was blacked out apart from the letter I was trying to read.

"No; they don't help, I can't read any more with these."

At that moment many thoughts raced through my mind.

"What! I don't believe it. That's all I can read? It's as bad as my left one."

"If your right eye is that bad, maybe your left is worse too."

"No way; I don't want to think about it."

"Can you swap and cover up your other eye please?" the doctor asked, breaking into my thoughts.

The moment had come to see or rather to find out if my left eye had deteriorated much. It was a very intense moment and I hesitated before covering up my right eye.

"Here goes," I thought hysterically.

"It's… it's…"

I blinked vigorously and tried to focus more clearly. Then I opened my eye wide and tried again.

"It's… too blurred. I can't read anything, not even the top line; the big letter on its own."

"Are you sure that you can't read anything?" the doctor asked.

I tried once more but was disappointed again. I felt a tear building up in my eye.

"No; nothing. I can't read anything; I can't believe it."

My heart sank and I became overwhelmed by emotions.

"My left eye can't see anything, what's happened to me?"

"What a great life you've got ahead of you."

"I hate my eyes, they're so useless. They can't even see enough to read anything. I hate them, I hate them and I hate my life."

"Can you see any clearer with the dark glasses on?" the doctor asked.

Nothing seemed clearer with them on. Everywhere was too dark and too distorted.

"Can you see me waving my hand?"

He began to wave his hand near my face to see if my eye had any response to movement.

"Yes, but it's not clear."

"Try this. I'm going to hold a card up and I want to know if you can read anything on it."

He held up a card and slowly walked forwards towards me until I was able to read it.

"Yes, I can read it but it still isn't clear."

"Thank you. Please follow me out to the waiting room."

After I found my seat my mind drifted as I struggled to fight off the conflicting thoughts.

The next test was my field test where I had to look into a satellite dish and signal whenever I could see a small light. Over the years I'd noticed that the light had become harder to see and reappeared less frequently. This test made it obvious that my eyesight had deteriorated further. I could almost feel the blind spots taking over my field of vision. It was clear to me that they were a lot worse and I almost became hysterical. After the doctor confirmed that the blind spots were increasing, the conflicting thoughts in my mind started once more.

"The blind spots are growing and it's only a matter of time before you go blind."

"No! I'm not going blind, I won't accept it. It's too much to cope with. This isn't happening to me. Why does my eyesight have to be so cloudy, why… why?"

I was sent back to the waiting room to await my next test. While sitting there I was almost in tears as my emotions got the better of me. I was ready to explode and I wanted to scream 'WHY ME!' but somehow I contained myself.

The next test was to check the pressure in my eyes and also to look at the back of my eyes with an ophthalmoscope for any obvious signs of deterioration. They checked the pressure first and then put some eye drops in to dilate my eyes to get a clearer look. Then I was sent to wait while the drops took effect. The world slowly became more distorted as pictures and people became harder to recognise.

"Here we go again. I hate this feeling. I'm worried about what it's going to be like if I go blind. It will be too much to cope with, I give up; life stinks."

"Think of something happy or positive."

"What's the point? Things are getting worse and I've run out of strength. You win. I give up. I haven't got the strength to fight any more."

Some tears appeared and began to run down my face. It was too much for me to comprehend and I sat there weeping.

My eyesight became so distorted that I had to be assisted back into the room, a nurse linked my arm and slowly guided me in and helped me to my seat. It made me feel so frail and useless. The doctor gave me a tissue to wipe away my tears and then proceeded to finish the test.

"There's a lot of scarring on the discs in your eyes," he said.

"I know; the doctor at the other Eye Hospital said that too."

"Do you experience problems with objects disappearing?"

"All the time; I can't see coins unless they're in my hand. If I drop money it disappears even though it could be right by my foot. Sometimes I get embarrassed having to ask someone else to find money that I've accidentally dropped in a shop. Also parts of people's faces are disappearing. Unless I'm standing right next to someone, they look like they have parts of their body missing. People look like ghosts and it's pretty scary to see."

"Do you have tunnel vision?"

"No; I don't think so. I see things fine if they're close to me and I see lots of light."

"What about at night?"

"I experience many problems at night-time. I've got night blindness."

"Yes; I know. Do you use eye drops?"

"Yes."

"There's quite a lot of pressure in your eyes. Do you do anything strenuous?"

"I used to lift heavy weights but I've stopped now. The last doctor told me that it was dangerous to put additional strain on my eyes."

"Do you experience any other problems?"

"Like what?"

"Is your vision cloudy?"

"Yes... why?"

"You have a small cataract in your eye which would give you cloudy vision. Your eyes are very dry and that would cause it too. I'll prescribe you some tear drops to moisten your eyes."

"Cataract? How did I get that? My eyes are bad enough, I don't need that too."

"It's only small, you should be fine."

"Why don't you operate on my eyes to get rid of the cloudy vision? It causes me so much distress; it would help me a great deal if you could at least give me clearer vision. It's horrible; it's like looking at everything through thick fog and the fog is getting denser."

"I'm sorry, but there's no way that we can touch your eyes. They're too delicate and we don't know enough about your eye disorder."

"I don't care any more. I want to see clearer. I've had enough of having bad eyesight so if you can get rid of the cloudy vision that would help a great deal."

"Use the tear drops and see if they make a difference."

I became very distressed. One by one more things were going wrong with my eyes and there was nothing that I could do about it. There was too much wrong with them now. It wasn't just one thing, there were several and I became emotional.

"I can't believe this. What's happening to my eyes? Why do they have to be so poor? It's too much to comprehend. It seems like everything is going wrong in my life."

When I entered another room for more tests there was only a doctor present. I was told that there were no more vigorous tests for me. The doctor was a specialist who had taken over from the professor. She introduced herself and then began reading my notes.

"Can I have a look at the back of your eyes?"

"Yes."

As she approached me a thought came into my mind.

"Why is everyone so fascinated with my eyes? It's like they've never seen my disorder before."

She then had a look at the back of my eyes with her ophthalmoscope.

"There's got to be something seriously wrong," I thought to myself. "This disorder is no longer new so they should know enough about it by now."

Then another thought came to me.

"Unless my disorder is new. They said that my sister shouldn't have had any problems, yet she seems to be losing her eyesight too."

Although I was feeling very emotional, I was also feeling confused.

"If my sister has RP and she shouldn't, then maybe we haven't got the strain of RP that they thought we had. Maybe they don't know what's wrong with our eyes. Maybe that's why they're so fascinated by what it looks like. I could be right because they're not sure why I'm also deaf. Well... I guess if they don't know what's wrong then I should be grateful that they're all so interested in finding out more."

She finished looking at my eyes and then asked me a few questions.

"Can you see my finger?"

She held up her hand and was waving some of her fingers to check if I could see them.

"I know that you're holding up your arm but I can't see your hand or any fingers. Your arm looks too blurred and you're too far away from me to see your hand."

She came closer until I was able to see.

"Can you see now?"

"Yes I can see your hand but not clearly."

"Keep your eyes focussed on my finger and follow wherever I move it."

When she moved her finger I stayed in the same position. Then I noticed that her arm had moved so that meant her finger must be somewhere else so I looked around until I focussed on it once more but every time she moved her finger I could feel a delay before I was able to see it again. She then sat back down to ask a few more questions.

"Yes, there's a long delay before you focus on things," she said.

"That's because I was struggling to see your hand, so I was watching the movements of your arm as it's much bigger and easier to see, even though it also appears blurred to me."

"Your eyesight is very poor."

"I know; that's why I'm here. Have you discovered a cure yet?"

"We will soon."

"Not for me though. I won't be cured. By the time you discover a cure, I'll be too old to care or already be dead. I'm more worried about our next generation just in case any of them get it."

"Are you working?"

"I'm a Computer Technician working with lots of small computer screens that cause me a great deal of distress."

"Have you any specialist equipment to help you manage?"

"Yes; I have a keyboard with large letters; a large monitor; magnification programs and a CCTV to help me read."

"Do you go out at night?"

"Sometimes but I struggle more at night to see. People have to be right next to me for me to be able to identify them and that still depends on the amount of light. Most of the time I guess, or recognise them from their voices. It's very frustrating but that's the only way that I see people."

"You've lost a great deal of vision and your eyes are showing lots of signs of tunnel vision."

"How much vision have I lost?"

"I would say… 95%."

"Pardon? Sorry, but how could I have such little vision and still be getting around so well?"

"I'm afraid that we're going to have to register you as blind."

For a minute I was lost for words as I tried to take in what she had just said.

"Your eyes have deteriorated considerably since your last appointment."

"Blind? But I can see."

"You can only see things that are very close to you. Many blind people can see a little. You don't have to be totally blind to be registered as blind."

"I don't want to be blind."

"Walk with me."

She walked off around the room and I followed. Then she went out of the door, along a corridor and back into the room and all the time she was watching my actions closely. It wasn't clear to me where she was going and I couldn't see if there were any obstacles in my way so I followed behind her carefully, rather than walking with her. We then returned to our seats.

"You see, you followed me, you didn't walk with me. You looked very unsure of your surroundings because it was all new to you. The way you walked like you were thinking so hard about each step, told me that you couldn't see."

"My sight isn't clear enough for me to walk beside people so I tend to follow then. I've done this for a long time and that's why people think that I can see more than I really can but I never dreamt that I've been walking around practically blind."

"You have and you're doing well but you need more help and I think that it's about time that you used a white stick. If you like I won't register you as blind if it upsets you, but you are and you can receive more help that you need."

I was in shock and hesitated before answering.

"Blind!" I thought to myself. "Oh my God, I'm blind! What am I going to do? I wasn't supposed to be blind, not yet. How will I ever cope? It's too much for me to handle. I can't be blind. I don't want to be blind. My whole life has just ended. I hated the feeling of imagining how it would be if I became blind and all this time I was already… blind. No, this is a dream – a nightmare. This isn't happening to me. No, I refuse to accept it."

My body was numb as I sat there wondering what to do and what to say.

"Shall I sign the form to say that I'm registered blind? How will I tell everyone? This is going to be so humiliating. I'll lose students at my Martial Arts club; nobody will want to train under a blind instructor. They'll say that I can't see if they're doing something right or wrong. I don't know what to do."

"Sign the form and accept help. You've done well to get this far on your own, now it's time to ask for help and to trust other people."

"Maybe I'll sign, but I'm not telling everyone, I can't, I can't take it, no, it's too embarrassing."

It took me a few moments while I contemplated what to do in my mind, but finally I made a decision.

"Yes, I'll sign the form to say that I'm now classed as blind," I answered, feeling defeated.

She approached me and showed me the form to sign.

"Where should I sign?" I asked.

"Here; where my finger is."

She even moved my hand to the right position so that my pen was near her finger.

"She's right; I can't see," I thought as I struggled to sign. "I'm fooling myself. How long haven't I been able to see? How long have I been blind without knowing?"

CHAPTER 10

I'm not a robot

The stress of knowing that I was now registered blind almost became unbearable. A serious battle was on the way to deter me from the thoughts that could render me helpless.

"I'm blind? I can't believe it. I can't see anything clearly. There's no way that I can go for my 4th Dan black belt now! Not now that I'm registered blind."

"You can't give everything up. You've worked too hard."

Then I became emotional.

"What's the point? Everywhere looks too blurred. I hate my eyes. I feel like an invalid."

Somehow I was able to convince myself to go out during the day using my white cane at its true length. On the way to town I passed people and was horrified with what I saw. They looked like their heads were missing. The ghostly figures of people were back and scarier than before. They now looked like ghosts with disfigured faces. Some of them appeared to be walking around without legs. The blind spots in my eyes were growing and my world was slowly disappearing.

After a while I came to a road that I had to cross. I stood and waited. A minute or so passed and I was still waiting for a clear gap in the traffic. It wouldn't have looked good if I rushed across, just missing a car, like I usually did, so I waited. Then I listened carefully with my good ear. It was difficult to identify all the blurred images. The air became almost silent and I couldn't see any obvious blurred images moving. The road appeared to be clear, but then I saw a bicycle pass. It appeared from nowhere. They were very hard for me to see because bikes are small compared to the larger blurred images of cars. They are also silent which also causes me additional problems. If I were to wait until I was sure that it was clear then I would be waiting all day. I had to take a risk so I held my breath and crossed hesitantly.

I came across another road and waited until I could hear that it was clear. That too made me think.

"I didn't realise that I used my hearing so much when I cross roads."

I held my breath and walked across quite hastily.

Once I was in the town centre one of my friends approached me.

"Hello. How are you?" they asked.

Their voice was familiar and I was able to decipher who they were. As we chatted I became confused with where to look. The disfigured ghostly figure that I saw of them horrified me. I attempted to hold a civil conversation at the same time as dismissing the conflicting thoughts that were growing in my mind.

"What's that stick for?"

"Here we go," I thought. "Surely they know what it's for, but I have to tell them I guess."

"I've got very bad eyesight and sometimes I need this cane," I replied.

I'd tried to say that I was registered blind but it wasn't ready to reveal itself.

Now I felt nervous but I knew that I had to reveal the true nature of my disability soon.

The next person I met I knew that I would have to tell them. I'd already told people that I was partially sighted but now I had to get used to telling people that I was now registered blind. After a brief chat I prepared myself for that awkward question.

"What's that for?" they asked.

"I have to use this cane now," I answered.

"Why? Has your eyesight got worse?"

"Yes… I'm registered blind now."

"Blind? But you saw me and you can see me now can't you?"

"No; you spoke first and I recognised you from your voice. That's how I knew that it was you."

"What do you see?"

"You appear to be wearing a mask. Unless you turn your face into the light, your features are too hard to identify and… you look like a ghost."

A tear came to my eye. It just appeared from nowhere. I didn't realise that I would feel so sad after explaining that I'm registered blind. I suddenly felt useless speaking about how bad my eyesight had become. As I walked on, I found myself explaining the same thing to another friend. Admitting that I was registered blind was draining me of my energy. It was making me feel worse than knowing the truth and pretending to others. Explaining to other people made me realise how bad my eyesight really was.

There were several situations that I struggled to deal with. A ghostly figure stopped to have a chat to me and I was unable to identify them from their voice.

"Do you know who I am?" the voice asked.

"No, I can't see properly," I answered.

"Maybe I should leave this cane at home next time," I thought to myself. "Some of my friends are ignoring it anyway. How am I supposed to recognise someone if I clearly can't see them?"

Maybe they weren't thinking straight when they asked the question but it still made me feel as though my white cane was invisible. Although I was a little upset with the situation, I also felt sorry for some of the people. It was obvious that they didn't know what to do or say to a blind person. Some of them had probably never come into contact with one before and it was a shock to their system. It was also partly my fault. I shouldn't be embarrassed of what I am and shouldn't get emotional having to explain my disability to others. It was all new to me too and I hoped that I would learn to deal with it but at that time I was a little angry at life.

When I got back home I became dizzy with thoughts. I tried to think of some happy memories; something positive that would take my mind off my problems.

Although I was put off going for my 4th Dan black belt exam due to my lack of eyesight, training was a great way of diverting my thoughts onto something positive. It was an outlet for all the anger and frustration that I was battling against. I found myself practising long and hard. I'm not sure how it happened but the more I practised the more energy I appeared to have. Sometimes I would go to the gym for a light session with my friend John who would help change the weights for me. At night-time I still wasn't tired so I would look for other things to do and would sometimes still be up at 2 am, pottering around my house, tidying up here and there and generally making myself useful while I still had the energy. I started to notice that I was losing weight easily but I put it down to the excessive training.

One day my sister from London, Carline, came to visit us in Rugby and saw how active I was. She complained that I had too much energy for someone who was doing so much during a typical day. She was a trained nurse and had only recently changed her job but she still had her skills of observation.

"Come here to me," she said.

"Why; what have I done now?" I asked.

"Nothing; I'm just curious. I want to have a look at your eyes."

"What for? I know that I can't see."

"No; I think that there's something else wrong, I sense it."

"More wrong? I think that I've had enough problems with my eyes to keep me going for years thanks."

"Let me look at your eyes," she insisted.

So I went closer and she made her diagnosis.

"Your eyes are bulging out. I've got a feeling that you've got a thyroid problem," she concluded.

"A what?" I asked, feeling worried.

"That could explain why you appear to have loads of energy. You're too active, something's definitely wrong," she answered.

"No; it's the pressure of my eyes from the glaucoma. My eyes are always in terrible pain from it, I've got eye drops to relieve some of the pressure."

"It could be but what about your weight loss? You look like you've lost a lot of weight lately."

"I've lost over 7kg, but that's because I train so hard."

"Why not make an appointment to see your doctor? Let him have a look at you."

I agreed and was referred to the Rugby St Cross Hospital to see a specialist called Doctor O'Hare.

The doctor called me into his room and began his tests. He read through the results of a recent blood test and also the results of my blood pressure and took my body weight. Then he had a look at my bulging eyes. He also felt around my neck for my glands and asked me to swallow. Then he asked me to hold out my hands. They were trembling slightly, I could feel them shaking but I thought that was because I was nervous. Then the questions started.

"Have you got an eye disorder?"

"Yes; I have RP and glaucoma and a small cataract."

"RP? That's fascinating. Can I take a look into your eyes?"

"Help yourself; everyone else does."

He looked at the back of my eyes with his ophthalmoscope and said, "Wow; it's incredible. It would be better if your eyes were dilated but they're very interesting."

"I've had more than my fair share of eye drops to dilate my eyes thanks."

He proceeded to ask about my eye condition before turning back to my immediate problem.

"You have hyperactive thyroids," he announced.

"How come?" I asked.

Through My Eyes

"There are many ways that they can flair up. Your heart is working too hard like you're constantly exercising and we need to slow it down before you have a heart attack. I'm going to prescribe you with two different tablets that will help to control them."

"Will I have to use them for the rest of my life?"

"Maybe."

At that moment I felt like I had gone into shock.

"More problems?" I thought to myself. "I'm now in danger of having a heart attack? I can't believe this is happening to me. I'm so lucky that Carline is a nurse and spotted it or I would still be racing around until all sorts of hours in the morning. Then I might have had a heart attack. I really am a misfit; my body is falling apart. I won't be donating any of my organs now, it wouldn't help anyone."

Doctor O'Hare told me that I would have to have regular appointments every four months to check that the amount of tablets were sufficient to slow me down and stabilise my thyroid.

When I got home I became confused.

"Why me? Why is all this happening to me? I'm registered blind, isn't that enough?"

"Think of happy thoughts. Don't get too emotional."

I became emotional, sad but angry at the same time. I knew that I had to conquer my emotions for fear of giving in to depression. It was a fight that I had to continue but the way things were going it would only be a matter of time before I exploded. I had plenty of emotions but hid them well. People still saw me with a smile on my face but underneath I was hurting and beginning to boil. When friends asked me for my opinion on things I would answer with an almost cold expression.

"Have you heard that your mate is in hospital with liver failure?" a friend asked me.

"He shouldn't drink so much alcohol," I replied without concern.

It was too difficult for me to explain to my friend what I've been through and what goes on in my head. I did have feelings, of course I did, but I knew that I had to learn how to control them or I would fall apart. Rather than trying to explain my actions and making myself feel upset from reliving the truth of how bad my eyesight was, I chose to ignore them and leave them to their own conclusions. Talking about what I see would lead me to become too emotional and that would be too much stress for me to cope with. I didn't want to be reminded of how poor my eyesight was so I became silent.

Over the next few months I felt myself slowing down. The tablets for my hyperactive thyroids sometimes made me fall asleep in the early evening. They were only short naps, but sleep it was. For a few years I was an insomniac and never realised it. There were so many different sports that I took part in and I thought that they were the reason why I had so much energy. It seemed that I'd had hyperactive thyroids for years and I'd never known. If it weren't for my sister warning me I would probably have had a heart attack. That scared me and added to my chain of thoughts. Then I had my second shock that year that deterred me from thinking about my thyroid problem.

My sister Angela, who had devoted her life to looking after our mother and us, came back with some crippling news. She had also been registered blind by the Birmingham Eye Hospital and was very upset and was finding the news hard to deal with. It was a shock to us all.

"I can't believe this," I thought. "Three of us, all registered blind, that's ridiculous. Why is this happening to us?"

She said the doctors told her that we all have a 50% chance of getting it. That's one in two of us so I became curious, wondering who else has it. Then a weird sensation came over me.

"If my sister can get it then… maybe my two children can. No… that's too much to think about, please no; not my children."

CHAPTER 11

Down but not out

Martial Arts was a great way of diverting my thought away from my increasing eye disorder. It was a way of keeping busy and doing something positive. I managed to enjoy training enough to pursue my goal to become a Master of Taekwondo. In July 1997 I passed my 4th Dan black belt grading exam and became the first registered blind Master of Taekwondo in England. A Grand Master from Korea congratulated me and said that I had achieved more than him because he could not have performed as well as I had without his sight. This shocked me as it was coming from someone that I admired and respected. It made me realise that I had nothing else to prove. At that moment I vowed never to take another grading exam and decided to concentrate my energy on finding ways of coping with my deteriorating eyesight.

After my eye appointment in 1999, it was obvious that my eyes were continuing to deteriorate. Although I expected to hear that they were worse, I was scared to find out by what degree. Both my eyes were no longer able to read anything from the eye test chart. The doctor held a card with a very large letter printed on it and moved slowly towards me until I was able to focus on it. It made me feel frail and useless.

"When is this punishment going to stop?" I thought to myself sadly.

I then became overwhelmed with emotions as tears came streaming down my face. Seeing through my eyes were now like looking through binoculars that were extremely out of focus. This was with my glasses on, blurred distorted images that were disturbing to see.

"I don't want to go totally blind," I thought to myself hysterically.

Then I had to see the specialist for the results of the tests. She read through my notes and gave me feedback from each individual test. I sat there as she ripped my life to shreds. Then came some shocking news that left me baffled. The specialist informed me that she had the results of my blood test. She concluded that I was suffering from Usher's Syndrome which results in people going both deaf and blind.

"I'm going to go both deaf and blind?" I thought to myself.

I became very sad and couldn't wait to get back home so that I could express my emotions in private.

The constant memory of not being able to read any letters on the chart at the Eye Hospital weighed me down. Whenever I was unable to do something due to my lack of sight, the memories of the blurred chart would come flooding back.

Although I had specialist equipment to help me at work, my struggles continued. Part of my job was to help other people on their computers but I was unable to see clearly enough to help them efficiently. Most of the time I stood beside people picturing what was on their screens in my mind and then tried to help them from memory. It was working less and less and I was beginning to make too many mistakes. The tasks that I was struggling with began to build up and I was having difficulty coping with the stress it was causing me.

"Why me? Why is this happening to me?"

A short while later my boss left and she was replaced with someone who I felt was less compassionate and understanding. Although he was told that I was registered blind, he urged me to do more difficult jobs. He asked me to read all the serial numbers of the computers myself even though I told him that I physically wouldn't be able to do it, but that I had prefects who could help me. He seemed to ignore my disability; he wanted me to do the job myself. After a short while he even took away my prefects so I had nobody to help me do the difficult jobs. There were many tasks that I was asked to perform and my job became too much again. I felt as though he was ignoring my disability and wanted me to do my job or leave.

"I can't do my job anymore," I thought to myself.

The pressure was on and a job that I had previously looked forward to doing became a nightmare – it became an extra strain on my mind and added to my problems. We argued and almost came to blows but he was my boss and had the power to influence other managers. After a while I felt as though I had to drag myself into work every day – I no longer looked forward to going there.

Around this time my sisters added to my emotional strain. Angela found a lump and was worried so she asked my other sister Carline to accompany her to the hospital for tests. Angela was fortunate and the lump turned out to be benign. While in the hospital, Carline decided that she might as well undergo tests too. She was less fortunate and was diagnosed with cancer. When she told us we were devastated. We couldn't believe that Angela was fine but Carline had cancer. It added to my growing depression and I was slowly becoming superstitious. I was now beginning to believe that our family was cursed.

"I can't take anymore pressure," I thought sadly.

Not being able to perform my job efficiently and the growing problems my family were experiencing finally became too much for me. My negative thoughts overpowered me and I had to make an appointment with my doctor. After I explained my feelings he decided to sign me off work with depression. He hoped that the break from my stress of not being able to cope with my job would relax me enough to put me in a more positive frame of mind.

A week soon became a month and I had not returned to work. I was still showing no signs of improvement and sank further into depression.

"I'm hopeless," I thought to myself pathetically. "I can't see clearly enough to do my job."

There were no words of encouragement in my mind and I sank deeper and deeper.

My doctor noticed the change in my personality and referred me to a psychiatric therapist. Sometimes I would attend my appointments and not smile or even unzip my coat. I no longer cared about anything or anyone. The one thing that I'd been trying so hard to avoid for so many years had finally won. Sometimes I would sit in almost silence and other times I would say a few words but my therapist slowly got me to open up and admit what was wrong. She avoided referring to my eyesight much. She would ask a few more questions each session until she found things that I enjoyed talking about – something to relight the positive fire that had accidentally been extinguished. As time went on, I became more relaxed about sharing my thoughts and problems with her.

"I feel like a failure," I sobbed. "My failing eyesight has prevented me from doing so much and now it's preventing me from doing my job."

She listened with compassion as I shared my dissatisfactions.

"Life isn't fair. How is anyone supposed to live a happy life without sight? We need our eyesight for virtually everything."

Several months had gone by and I was still not well enough to return to work. She soon worked out what used to make me happy and spoke about that more in hope of re-establishing a connection. Sometimes she would make a suggestion and other times she made me feel less pressured to try things.

"Why not try going to the gym once and if you feel too uncomfortable then feel free to return home."

After a while I tried out a session at my local gym. I had to force myself to go because my burning desire had faded. It wasn't easy but it had to be done. I had a choice to stay down and depressed or to fight to get back on my feet. Within ten minutes I felt some energy returning to me and it almost brought a smile back to my face.

The slight raise in my energy level opened me up to answer some more crucial questions.

"How would you feel returning to your job part-time?" she asked.

"That would make me feel even more like a failure."

The stress of not being able to cope at work added to my ability to deal with my lack of eyesight. It was obvious to my therapist that something had to go and it was only a matter of time before I admitted it.

"Deep down in your heart, what are you feeling?"

"I would feel better if I never had the stress of my job to think about. The constant reminder that I'm a failure is haunting me. I'm not sure if I can ever face going back."

At my next appointment I finally gave my decision about my job. It was too much for me so I decided to resign. It relieved me from a great deal of pressure and gave me more time to learn how to embrace my disability. Sharing thoughts about my eyes became easier and slowly I returned to the gym on a more frequent basis.

The more I exercised, the more positive I felt. This then led me to see a brighter side to life. As time went on I slowly came out of my depression.

"How are you feeling," She asked.

"I feel as though a huge weight has been lifted off my shoulders," I replied with a smile.

Then came the news that I'd been waiting for.

"It sounds like you have a firm grip on life again," she said.

"Yes; there will be times when I'll be down but I'll bounce back. I keep telling myself that there are people out there worse off than me. That makes me feel more fortunate again."

"I can say that you're no longer depressed."

"Thanks!" I said ecstatically.

"If you ever feel that you're getting down again, please don't leave it too late to make another appointment. Don't wait until you're too low because that's when you won't want to listen to other people's advice that will help you."

"Thank you for helping me get back on my feet to face the challenges of life."

I left my therapist and returned home. For several months I had suffered from depression but now, I was back!

CHAPTER 12

I'm blessed too

Feeling more outgoing, I decided to respond to a request to have my Martial Arts club travel to Germany for a friendly competition. Rugby twins with a town called Ruesselsheim in Germany and we agreed to represent the Martial Arts in the sports twinning. My students wanted to go by aeroplane so I had to overcome my fear of flying to be able to go. I'd never been on an aeroplane before but finally I agreed to go.

All was arranged and we set off. There were twelve of us and we travelled in three cars to London. Then we left our cars in a short stay car park where they could remain for the four days that we would be away. As soon as we arrived the questions started. I had only told certain people about the extent of my disability so there were a few students who didn't know. As I stepped out of the car into unknown territory, I opened my cane to its full length.

"What's that for?" a student asked.

"I've got very poor eyesight and I need to use this sometimes."

"How bad are your eyes?"

"I'm partially sighted," I replied.

"How can you see to teach us?"

We made our way to the shuttle bus where we lined up to get on.

Once we got to the Airport one of my black belt students called Katie, who was already aware of my disability helped me manoeuvre around objects and guided me up and down steps.

"This is a little embarrassing," I thought, "I'm the Instructor yet I'm the one being guided like an invalid."

We booked in and went to wait for our flight to arrive.

Once I boarded the aeroplane and got strapped in, I remembered that I was afraid of flying. Gradually I began to get nervous.

The engines started up and the aeroplane began to move as it taxied into position at the start of the runway. After a while it began to speed up. I closed my eyes like a big baby and prayed. The engine noise increased to a roar as the plane began to accelerate and my head was thrown back with the force. It felt like a rocket. My heart was pumping hard and I was very scared. Then it lifted off the ground and I became frantic. After a moment or two we levelled out, the engine noise subsided a bit and all was calm.

After two hours we prepared for landing. This felt worse than the take off. The aeroplane was shaking violently and I was praying again. The plane leaned from left to right as it prepared to land. It seemed to take forever to touch the ground and I wasn't sure how much more excitement I could take. I wanted my feet back on solid ground and to get out of there. Then things felt even worse. The aeroplane touched down and now the runway felt too rough and we shook even more. I thought that it would never stop, but just as I began to feel hysterical, everywhere went calm again and we travelled slowly towards the terminal. Landing was one of the scariest experiences I'd ever had.

In June 2002, my fun was cut short as I was given the shattering news of my sister Carline's health. She had been diagnosed with cancer some while before and had now been told that she had less than a year to live. All my family were devastated by the news. It seemed as though every time I tried to keep myself happy, something else would go wrong in my life.

Through My Eyes

Percy organised a family meeting and we discussed Carline's care. Many of my brothers and sisters were too busy with their own lives and occasionally visited her when they could find time. Percy was already looking after her everyday, cooking, cleaning, nursing and trying to help her become more comfortable. He asked us to share his workload because he was under a lot of pressure dealing with her mostly by himself. He even postponed a Social Economics course to dedicate more time to nursing her. I agreed to look after her every Thursday and hoped that it would also give Percy a rest from his stressful duties. June and Angela also volunteered for other days.

Angela became even more upset because she couldn't do more for her sister. For years she had enjoyed her independence and was looked up to as the older and wiser sister. She used to help everyone and was especially close to Carline. They did everything together but now Angela's eyesight had deteriorated to a much worse condition than mine, with no vision at all in her right eye and her left as blurred as mine. It seemed that the deterioration of her sight had accelerated and she was feeling frantic wondering when her left eye would become totally blind too. She so badly wanted to do more for Carline but was not physically capable.

On a Thursday I would look after Carline before and after teaching. Cooking in someone else's kitchen was difficult for me. Sometimes I would cook at my home and take the food that I had prepared to her. One day I asked Carline what type of food she liked the most and would like more of. She told me that her favourite was Chinese food, and particularly liked pork fried rice with sweet and sour sauce, so I agreed to buy her a Chinese meal every Thursday. It felt good to be able to please her but I knew that part of my relief was due to not having to struggle to cook for her. It was stressful not knowing how many months I would be able to please her before she grew too ill to eat.

During Christmas 2002 Carline told everyone that she wanted to make it a special one because she knew that it was going to be her last. We all spent Christmas at my home and tried to make it very special for her – it was a very emotional time for us all. Carline bought special presents for all her nieces and nephews including my two children – she bought Jasmine her first Bratz doll and car. (Jasmine now has over twenty Bratz!) Carline also spoilt her son Hasani, who was then twelve years old. She tried her best to keep a smile on her face as she treated all the children but we could all tell that she was in a great deal of pain. She was also on a very high dose of morphine.

I found it difficult to hide my real feelings and emotions towards the situation. While I was caring for her on my Thursday evenings I would battle within my mind to remain positive. My thoughts would drift from finding ways to cope with going blind and finding ways to accept that I was about to lose a sister to cancer.

In January 2003, Carline became even worse. Percy was already staying overnight to look after her and he was struggling. He said that he needed more help so I offered to stay overnight on Thursdays too. We slept in the sitting room. I usually got the privilege of sleeping upright on a sofa chair, which caused me some back pains that I didn't need because of my teaching career but I was able to cope. Percy also began to suffer backache but his was more severe than mine. My emotions began to build up as time went on and my sister became worse. Sometimes I would sit there watching TV with tears in my eyes.

During a conversation with Carline she told me that she had suffered a small stroke and temporarily lost her eyesight. She tried to tell me that she felt fortunate not to be registered blind like her three family members. I became emotional, tearful and confused to a degree that tears were constantly in my eyes.

"How can she say that she's fortunate not to be blind?" I thought to myself. "I'm blind and it's incredibly hard, but I'm not dying from cancer. I should be grateful to be blind; I'm not the one who only has a few months to live. The problem with my eyesight is bad, painful and stressful but she's worse off than me. At least I have a chance to live my life. She has to prepare herself for death. That sounds scarier than wondering when I'll finally go totally blind."

We confused each other as I tried my hardest to get her to understand that I was the lucky one. She kept saying that she had enjoyed a good life being able to see everything she wanted. She told me how fortunate she was to have had the ability to drive, walk and see the world. Although I would have loved to do some of the things that she had done if I could see more clearly, I still wouldn't prefer a short life.

A few months went by and her condition continued to deteriorate. She was now struggling to eat, but she still insisted on having her weekly Chinese.

Carline told Percy that she was afraid of what it might do to her son's mental health if he found her dead one morning, so we made sure that someone was always there with Hasani when he got up. There were a few helpers who also assisted her but she preferred her family. Carline also told us that she was afraid to fall into a deep sleep because she was afraid of dying and she wasn't ready to go yet.

Carline was strong willed but her illness slowly got the better of her and it got to a stage where she could no longer eat, talk or walk. We kept going to her house to nurse her and waited for the day when she would never wake up. Things were very quiet during my last Thursday night of nursing her. My nerves were on edge and I too was afraid of finding her dead but I had to be strong for the others.

On the Friday morning I prepared myself to leave her home. The doctor told Percy that he felt that she was about to pass away so Percy contacted every member of our family so that we could all be with her. We were all there, all together, waiting and worrying. During the afternoon we surrounded her bed to say our goodbyes. We watched as her breathing became fainter and she slowly slipped away from us. She had passed away with us all there. I cried that day.

For six months we had nursed her not knowing when she would leave us. She finally passed away on Friday 6th June 2003, aged forty-six.

CHAPTER 13

Now I can see

I knew that my eyesight was getting worse and that there wasn't much difference between what I saw with my glasses on or off. Soon I would no longer need to wear my glasses so I felt like I was now in a rush and running out of time to be able to see things. It was time to learn to deal with my sight loss.

The changes started with brushing my teeth. I often missed the toothbrush when trying to squeeze the toothpaste onto it, so I started spreading the toothpaste on one of my fingers, and then I smudged the toothpaste that was on my finger onto my teeth. Then I brushed them as normal but I washed the toothpaste off my finger first! I stopped looking in the mirror so that I didn't see a blurred image of myself as that usually created negative thoughts. There were many things that I avoided so that I didn't have so much chance to feel hopeless.

Somehow I learnt to control my OCD to a certain degree. I ignored most of the mess my children left. By avoiding looking at it or thinking about the problems it caused me by having to manoeuvre around toys, it slowly became easier to cope with. When I ate I tried not to look at my food unless I was using other parts of my eyes to see it. When I ate breakfast cereal I placed one of my fingers into the bowl so that I could feel how much milk I was pouring in. When I made a cup of tea, I held my cup over the sink. This way any spilt water went in the sink and not on the worktop. I also got in touch with Warwickshire association for the blind and they had many useful tools to also help me around the house. One very useful tool was a small raised dot that sticks on buttons on the microwave, cocker or washing machine. When I had toast and butter, I put the lid of the butter down somewhere that was a completely a different colour to it. It was a regular problem that I had because the lid seemed to disappear on the worktop, as it seemed to be of the same colour.

Most of the time I began to avoid eye contact with people because if I don't look, I don't think so much about my visual impairment. Sometimes I missed looking at people and would look at them using my central vision when the lighting was better. When I spoke to people I looked at them from the side of my eyes more because I seem to have more vision from the side. So when I appeared not to be looking at someone, I probably was and when I looked directly at them using my central vision in poor light, I couldn't actually see them. It feels cool sometimes because it's amazing how much more people look at you when they think that you're not looking at them.

Using my computer was still causing me stress. The keyboard began to look more cloudy and distorted so I found that I was pressing the wrong keys more often. Large text on my screen also became very difficult to see so I began to use magnification and speech software more regularly. Sometimes I amazed other people, especially my children, who could be struggling to manoeuvre around the computer screen and then I'd come along and do it with greater speed. I've switched off the screen and impressed my children by finding saved work solely using the speech software. It helped but I still struggled with the Internet so I hardly used it any more – most websites are not visual impaired friendly. Printing was another challenge. It was difficult for me to see if my work had printed correctly and colour prints were my greatest problem because I couldn't see colours like yellow, so my children agreed to check them for me. There have been many occasions when I thought that a coloured printout looked fine, but when my children checked it, they said otherwise.

When I went out at night for a drink I usually gave my money to a trusted friend to purchase my drinks from the bar. This prevented both hearing and eyesight confusion especially when there was blaring music in the background. I avoided going to the shop when there were other people around. I was slowly asking for more help; my friends read my letters for me and dealt with paperwork that I was unable to see clearly enough to deal with myself. My children wrote my cheques and I also asked my friends for more lifts when I felt uncomfortable walking but I still wasn't asking as much as I should. It wasn't easy; it's never easy – I knew that I had a choice to become depressed or to become strong.

I know that my days of holding onto what little vision I have left are drawing to a close. Most days now I'm finding it harder to persuade myself to go out. During the day my eyesight is very cloudy and out of focus; as time has gone on I've seen how objects slowly blend into each other and then disappear. I constantly see as though I'm looking through thickening fog and it becomes more noticeable as each month goes by. I'm finding it difficult to see the difference between the pavement and the road, the colours of most cars, lamp posts and boulders. Now people seem to have blended into the background to such an extent that I can hardly notice that someone is there unless they're moving close to me. Most of the time I'm now using every last part of my eyes where blind spots have yet to take over. This means my eyes have to dart around from left to right and in all directions to help me focus on something. While I'm doing this I'm also trying my best to constantly dismiss the thoughts from my mind that will lead to me feeling emotional.

Getting out of my bed is getting more difficult as my eyesight deteriorates. Sometimes I have to force myself to attend the gym. After ten minutes or so of exercise, the energy inspires me to want to carry on.

Choosing what to think about has become a habit. We tend to be controlled by our automatic thoughts and reactions but we can learn to control them and control our actions. If I have a negative thought in my mind then I battle to create positive ones to fill my head so I hardly think of the negative one. The more I think of something else rather than my original thought, the easier it becomes. It's a habit that I've created and it seems to work well.

We can choose what to think and we have a choice of what path we take. We all have problems – that's life. There are always other people worse off than us and I think about that all the time. Maybe if we stopped being so selfish and thinking that we are the only one with problems we could all learn to enjoy life more.

A friend of mine once told me that he had serious problems and moaned about them a lot. After a while I told him to thank God that his problems were not as bad as other people's. I also told him to try and enjoy his life while he could and not take anything for granted. He then asked me what I knew about problems because he didn't think that I had any. He had forgotten that I'm registered blind and don't advertise the problems that blind people experience, every minute of everyday so… I reminded him. After my short lecture on some of the obstacles I have had to get over on the way to dealing with my disability, he apologised. Just because people go around with a smile on their face and refrain from moaning, doesn't mean that they haven't got problems. I'm a good listener when someone has a serious problem, but I admit that I don't like listening to people moaning about trivial things. It causes me unnecessary stress and I normally switch off. I wasn't born strong or born able to cope with problems; I have persistently and consistently worked at it and shaped my personality.

Sometimes the person I'm with might comment on someone's facial features and a thought passes through my mind.

"They don't know how lucky they are being able to see that clearly. Maybe if they temporarily lost their sight they might appreciate that person for their personality and not their appearance."

It's in situations like this that I realise that I can see. I see when someone is kind and helpful or has a great personality – I can see people for who they truly are.

There are times where the lighting is great or the sun reflects off someone's face so that I'm able to see their features slightly clearer. It's at moments like these that you can catch me staring at people. It could be a male or a female friend, it doesn't matter, I'm just grateful to be able to see them. It doesn't matter how attractive they are or not, I'm thankful to God to be able to see them at that time because I know that most of the time I see people's faces as shadows. It's like a blessing for me to have these brief moments.

When I'm on my own I'll have the radio on or music channels on the TV. Anything that uses less sight to understand creates fewer thoughts in my confused mind. Music is beautiful and generally encourages positive thoughts in me. I listen to music a lot. One way that I flood out negative thoughts in my mind is to imagine that I'm listening to my favourite tracks or artists. Michael Jackson is my favourite, but there are many more musical artists who I admire. I sometimes get emotional when I listen to Stevie Wonder, but I really do admire him because his achievements have far surpassed mine and he has less vision than me. Compared to him, I can see. With the correct lighting I can see the difference between black and white. I can see red and sometimes yellow in bright light. I can see people's eyes, nose and mouth if the lighting is right. When I think of Stevie Wonder I realise how lucky I am.

There have been a few times where I've shocked a few people. These are some of the thoughts I have to cheer me up and bring a smile back to my face. I was standing waiting to use the pedestrian crossing when I sensed that the man next to me was struggling more than I was to cross the road. I listened carefully and realised that he was blind.

"Would you like some help crossing over the road?" I asked.

"Yes please," he replied.

"Hold onto me," I said.

"Thank you; you're very kind."

"You wouldn't trust me if I told you my little secret," I said jokingly.

After we got across to the other side he turned to me and asked; "What's your secret then?"

"I'm blind too," I answered.

"I couldn't tell," he said.

"I don't tell many people and I follow where other people walk so that it appears as though I can see," I replied.

"How are you able to get around so well?"

"I force myself to come out regularly so that I learn where most of the obstacles are."

He seemed to know where he was going from there so I left him. My friend who I was with was in hysterics.

"Well that really was the blind leading the blind," he said.

That wasn't the only time it happened. There was also another elderly man struggling to cross a road. I wasn't sure whether he was blind or not and I was going to pass him but decided to observe his movements a little more closely.

"Can you help me?" he asked.

"Yes, of course I can," I replied.

"Most people see me struggling and walk right past me."

"I was going to do that too," I thought to myself jokingly.

"They are inconsiderate people," I said.

"Can you guide me to the bank please?" he asked.

"I struggle to find the glass door too," I thought to myself.

"Yes, no problem," I answered.

He was very grateful and I never told him that I was registered blind too. I thought that maybe he would have run a mile and not trusted me to guide him.

There was another incident that sometimes makes me laugh when I think about it. I was out using my white cane (properly) and a car pulled up beside me.

"Excuse me, but can you help me?" a voice asked.

When I stopped to see what the problem was, I was surprised to hear that they were lost and were asking me for directions. The funniest thing was that I managed to point them in the right direction. I will always be confused with why they would select a blind person to ask for directions.

My friend Zack guided me once and we ended up in hysterics. It was at night and in an area that I wasn't used to so I felt disorientated. There were few streetlights and I kept thinking that I was about to bump into something. Zack kept telling me that I was nowhere near a lamp post but I felt unsafe. He then linked my arm as though we were married and he led me towards the restaurant. Zack told me that several cars stopped and the drivers and passengers were having a good long look at us, obviously thinking that we were gay. Zack is a muscular man (like myself!) and together we appeared to be two big strong gay blokes. We laughed in hysterics as people continued to wonder in their sick minds.

After twenty years of Martial Arts I have come to the point where I hardly ever kick. This is because I have many young students and I can hardly see them so I don't want to accidentally kick them. It feels great to encourage and inspire other people in achieving more. My students get a badge for doing well. The badges become sweets over the Christmas season. It's an incentive that I use that seems to work well, especially with my younger students. I can almost magically get students to try harder. What I do is purposely give a badge to someone and then I watch all the rest trying harder as they attempt to gain a badge too. They receive badges for being disciplined, trying extra hard, becoming flexible and fighting with effort. I watch shy people become confident and people with introverted personalities become outgoing and great leaders. I encourage students to believe that they are better than they think they are. I try my best to pass on my positive attitude and after a while they believe it too and become more confident. I change the lives of many people and that makes me feel as though I'm doing something worthwhile.

Life is too short and we need to find ways to enjoy it because we never know when our time will be up. Stop looking for Mr Perfect when you already have Mr Right. We all have something we would like to improve about ourselves so we need to think differently about people. Don't let your thoughts control you. Try to control your mind. I do have emotions but I've learnt to control them well. Sometimes it's nice to cry but I don't stay emotional for long – I avoid things that make me feel too emotional.

For years I've been used as a guinea pig for postgraduates who may become doctors. I've sat there while so many of them look into my eyes using their ophthalmoscopes and I hope, I hope and pray that one of them will look into my eyes and see their way to discovering a cure. It might not be for me but at least the next generation of RP suffers may have a cure. It might happen one day but I'll not wait. I can enjoy my life with what little vision I have left.

My low vision has opened up my eyes to see people for who they are and not for what they look like. At long last I understand what my father meant when he told me that I would be able to see. He didn't mean with my eyes.

You only have one life. Life is the greatest gift, so cherish it instead of wasting it.

ABOUT THE AUTHOR

Vendon Wright was born on the sixth of August 1966 in a small town called Rugby in England. He was registered blind at the age of twenty-eight, after a ten year battle. He suffers from Retinitis Pigmentosa (RP), a rare eye disorder that slowly destroys the pigment cells in the eyes. So far, there are no known cures. Battling against such a crippling disease led him through a labyrinth of challenges. His fight to remain positive was put under more pressure when he found out that he was also suffering from Usher syndrome, a disorder that results with him going both deaf and blind.

His journey involved experiencing a wide range of emotions which was necessary in order to deal with his disability. The issues and challenges became so intense that it brought him to a crossroad where he had the choice to give up fighting against such a crippling medical condition or to continue on his struggles. It was at this point where he became a Christian and now believes that God is with him through all his struggles. After a long hard battle of overcoming huge obstacles, he finally learned to embrace his medical condition.

OTHER BOOKS

I was blind but now I can see

One a day

Printed in Great
Britain
by Amazon